Istanbul Tourism, Turkey

The History and Travel Information, a Guide

Author
Caleb Gray.

SONITTEC PUBLISHING. All rights reserved. No part of this publication may be reproduced, distributed, or transmitted in any form or by any means, including photocopying, recording, or other electronic or mechanical methods, without the prior written permission of the publisher, except in the case of brief quotations embodied in critical reviews and certain other noncommercial uses permitted by copyright law. For permission requests, write to the publisher, addressed "Attention: Permissions Coordinator," at the address below.

Copyright © 2019 Sonittec Publishing
All Rights Reserved

First Printed: 2019.

Publisher:
SONITTEC LTD
College House, 2nd Floor
17 King Edwards Road,
Ruislip
London
HA4 7AE

Table of Content

SUMMARY 1
INTRODUCTION 5
   LANDSCAPE 7
      City site 7
      Climate 8
      City layout 9
      Architecture 13
         Byzantine monuments 13
         Turkish monuments 18
HISTORY 23
   EARLIEST TIMES 23
   DECLINE OF ROME & THE RISE OF CONSTANTINOPLE 28
   JUSTINIAN & THEODORA 31
   UNDER SIEGE & IN DECLINE 33
   THE CRUSADERS: INTERLOPERS FROM THE WEST 35
   THE OTTOMANS: UPSTARTS FROM THE EAST 38
   THE CONQUEST 40
   THE CITY ASCENDANT 42
   RULE OF THE WOMEN 44
   DECLINE, THEN ATTEMPTS AT REFORM 46
   ETHNIC NATIONALISM 47
   ABDÜL HAMIT II & THE YOUNG TURKS 49
   REPUBLICAN ISTANBUL 51
   DOWNGRADED: NO LONGER THE CAPITAL 52
   THE COUP YEARS 54
   THE RECENT PAST 55
CULTURAL LIFE 59
TRAVEL AND TOURISM 62
   TRAVELING TO ISTANBUL GUIDE 64
      Coming in to Istanbul 64
         Visa requirements 64
         Coming by plane 66
         Coming by train 72
         Coming by bus 75
         Coming by Boat 77
         Coming by Var 77
   QUICK ACTIVITIES GUIDE 79

- Getting around inside Istanbul 138
  - Public transport 138
  - Istanbulkart 140
  - By bus 143
  - By metro 145
  - By tram 149
- Things to Do in Istanbul 163
- Places to See in Istanbul 165
- Things to do in Istanbul 171
  - Sultanahmet Travel Guide 174
    - Turkish and Islamic Arts Museum 176
  - Taksim Travel Guide 178
  - Beyoglu Travel Guide 180
  - Galata Istanbul 184
  - Bosphorus 187
  - Anadolu Kavagi, last stop of Bosphorus ferry and Yoros Castle Istanbul 189
  - Prince's Islands Istanbul 191
  - Kadikoy Travel Guide 193
  - Moda Travel Guide 196
  - Halic (Golden Horn) Istanbul, Fener, Balat, Eyup Sutluce 198
  - Bebek Travel Guide 200
  - Ortakoy Travel Guide 203
  - Besiktas Travel Guide 207
  - Eminonu Travel Guide 210
  - Uskudar Travel Guide 213
  - Bagdat Street Istanbul 217
  - Camlica Hill Istanbul 218
- Interesting facts about Istanbul 219
- Istanbul Restaurant Guide 225
- Istanbul Nightlife 238
- Events and Festivals in Istanbul 239
- Climate 241

Summary

The importance of travelling in our life?

Everyone has their very own reasons to travel. Some people travel for work, some travel for pleasure while for others it is just a way of life. They travel to live and to escape at the same time.

Whatever might be the reason to travel, here are few ways in which travelling would definitely change you and I think that is why travelling becomes so important in life:

<u>Enjoy being alone</u>: There is something therapeutic about being alone and being at peace with it. While you soak in a new culture, you also connect with your own inner self.

<u>Learn to adapt</u>: It is a different world out there, literally. Be it the pace of life, the language or simply the change in weather, it is always a change and you have to adapt to it. This is what makes travelling truly beautiful as you break away from the routine and adapt to something totally new.

<u>Experience a new culture</u>: Every place comes with its distinct cultural habits, you cannot think about New York without talking about its fast paced life and about Italy without enjoying its relaxed lifestyle. Similarly, while visiting the UK you might have to be a bit formal in your interactions with the locals, on the other hand, while greeting the people in Thailand, one can be really warm and casual.

<u>Broaden your taste buds</u>: Travelling without experiencing the local food is just not complete. It is not only a culinary experience but a cultural one as well.

<u>Get out of comfort zone</u>: From simple experiences like the weather, way of life or food to the more adventurous ones like trying a new sport, travelling really pushes ones boundaries to the core. You might end up participating in a street carnival in Brazil just like the locals or trying the local delicacies (read insects) in Thailand.

<u>Indulge in Photography</u>: It does not matter whether you are a professional or not. It is also irrelevant whether you have a DSLR or a very basic camera, while travelling what matters is the love and quest for seeing beautiful places and the sheer joy of capturing them in your lense. Travelling would in return give you your very own collection of amazing postcards of beautiful sunsets, snow laced mountains or sunny beaches.

<u>Learn to escape</u>: Travelling is the best way to break the routine. If you are in a bustling city, go ahead and experience the country life. If you are in a rural place, travel to a bustling city and experience its madness.

Stressed with the city life or work pressure? A spa break in Himalayas or Kerala is a must try.

Appreciate Nature: The quest to explore more when one is travelling always leads to a sense of amazement about nature. While most of us keep a track of technological advancements, Nature has its own ways of outshining all of these. The Antelope Canyon in Arizona or Turquoise Ice in Russia are the finest examples of this. For more, check out the most unbelievable places around the world.

Get closer to your own roots: While one travels and experiences a lot of different cultures and practices, it definitely brings one closer to his or her own roots. Travel helps one appreciate one's identity and culture.

Travelling is all about experiences. They can happen in terms of culture, people, places but most importantly with one's own self and this was all about

Introduction

Istanbul, Turkish İstanbul, formerly Constantinople, ancient Byzantium, largest city and seaport of Turkey. It was the capital of both the Byzantine Empire and the Ottoman Empire.

The old walled city of Istanbul stands on a triangular peninsula between Europe and Asia. Sometimes as a bridge, sometimes as a barrier, Istanbul for more than 2,500 years has stood between conflicting surges of religion, culture, and imperial power. For most of those years it was one of the most coveted cities in the world.

The name Byzantium may derive from that of Byzas, who, according to legend, was leader of the Greeks from the city of Megara who captured the peninsula from pastoral Thracian tribes and built the city about 657 BCE. In 196 CE, having razed the town for opposing him in a civil war, the Roman emperor Septimius Severus rebuilt it, naming it Augusta Antonina in honour of his son. In 330 CE, when Constantine the Great dedicated the city as his capital, he called it New Rome. The coinage, nevertheless, continued to be stamped Byzantium until he ordered the substitution of Constantinopolis. In the 13th century Arabs used the appellation Istinpolin, a "name" they heard Byzantines use *eis tēn polin* which, in reality, was a Greek phrase that meant "in the city." Through a series of speech permutations over a span of centuries, this name became Istanbul. Until the Turkish Post Office officially changed the name in 1930, however, the city continued to bear the millenary name of Constantinople. Pop. (2007) 10,757,327; (2014 est.) urban agglom., 14,025,646.

Landscape

City site

The old city contains about 9 square miles (23 square km), but the present municipal boundaries stretch a great deal beyond. The original peninsular city has seven hills, requisite for Constantine's "New Rome." Six are crests of a long ridge above the Golden Horn; the other is a solitary eminence in the southwest corner. Around their slopes are ranged many of the mosques and other historic landmarks that were collectively designated a UNESCO World Heritage site in 1985.

By long tradition, the waters washing the peninsula are called "the three seas": they are the Golden Horn, the Bosporus, and the Sea of Marmara. The Golden Horn is a deep drowned valley about 4.5 miles (7 km) long. Early inhabitants saw it as being shaped like a deer horn, but modern Turks call it the Haliç ("Canal"). The Bosporus (İstanbul Boğazı) is the channel connecting the Black Sea (Karadeniz) to the Mediterranean (Akdeniz) by way of the Sea of Marmara (Marmara

Denizi) and the straits of the Dardanelles. The narrow Golden Horn separates old Istanbul (Stamboul) to the south from the "new" city of Beyoğlu to the north; the broader Bosporus divides European Istanbul from the city's districts on the Asian shore Üsküdar (ancient Chrysopolis) and Kadıköy (ancient Chalcedon).

Like the forces of history, the forces of nature impinge upon Istanbul. The great rivers of Russia and middle Europe the Danube, Don, Dnieper, and Dniester make the Black Sea colder and less briny than the Mediterranean. The Black Sea waters thrust southward through the Bosporus, but beneath them the salty warm waters of the Mediterranean push northward as a powerful undercurrent running through the same channel.

Climate

The prevailing northeast wind, or *poyraz*, comes from the Black Sea, giving way at times during the winter to an icy blast from the Balkans known as the *karayel*, or "black veil," capable of freezing the Golden Horn and even the Bosporus. The *lodos*, or southwest wind, can raise storms on the Sea of Marmara.

City layout

Fire, earthquake, riot, and invasion have ravaged Istanbul many times, more than 60 conflagrations and numerous earthquakes being important enough to have been recorded in history. The traces of these disasters, though, have been swept away in waves of intensive urban development: today wide roadways run through the historic quarters of the old city, and unpaved alleys overhung with old wooden houses coexist with modern high-rise buildings, office parks, and shopping malls.

Portions of the walls of Stamboul remain. The land walls, which isolate the peninsula from the mainland, were breached only once, by cannon of the Ottoman sultan Mehmed II (the Conqueror) in 1453, at the spot since called Cannon Gate (Top Kapısı). The walls are 4.5

miles (7 km) long and consist of a double line of ramparts the inner built in 413, the outer in 447 protected by a moat. The higher inner wall is about 30 feet (9 metres) high and 16 feet (5 metres) thick and is studded with 60-foot (18-metre) towers about 180 feet (55 metres) apart. Of 92 turrets originally raised on the outer wall, 56 are still standing.

The sea walls were built in 439. Only short sections of their 30-foot- (9-metre-) high masonry still remain along the Golden Horn. Intact, these walls had 110 towers and 14 gates. The walls along the Sea of Marmara, which stretch about 5 miles (8 km) from Seraglio Point, curving around the bottom of the peninsula to join the land walls, had 188 towers; they were, however, only about 20 feet (6 metres) high, because the Marmara currents provided good protection against enemy landings. Most of these walls still stand.

Within the city walls are the seven hills, their summits flattened through the ages but their slopes still steep and toilsome. Geographers number them from the seaward tip of the peninsula, proceeding inland along the Golden Horn, the last hill standing alone where the land walls reach the Sea of Marmara.

The Galata and Atatürk bridges cross the Golden Horn to Beyoğlu. Each day before dawn their centre spans are swung open to allow passage to seagoing ships. The shores of the Horn, served by water buses, are a jumble of docks, warehouses, factories, and occasional historical ruins. Ferries to the Asian side of Istanbul leave from under the Galata Bridge. Istanbul has three of the world's longest suspension bridges: Bosporus I (Boğazici) Bridge (completed in 1973), with a main span of 3,524 feet (1,074 metres); Bosporus II, the Fatih Sultan Mehmed Bridge (1988), 3,576 feet (1,090 metres); and Bosporus III, the Yavuz Sultan Selim Bridge (2016), 4,620 feet (1,408 metres). Two tunnels under the Bosporus, one for passenger rail and one for automobile traffic, were opened in 2013 and 2016 respectively.

Beyoğlu, considered to be "modern Istanbul," remains, as it has been since the 10th century, the foreign quarter. Warfare and fires have left standing only a few structures that were built earlier than the 19th century. The approach from the Golden Horn is steep, and a funicular railway runs between the Galata waterfront and the Pera Plateau. On the heights are the big hotels and restaurants, the travel bureaus, theatres, the opera house, the consulates, and many Turkish government offices.

From the 10th century onward, Galata was an enclave for foreign traders principally the Genoese who enjoyed extraterritorial privileges behind their walls. After the Ottomans took the city in 1453, all foreigners who were not citizens of the empire were restricted to this quarter. Around palatial embassies were compounds that included schools, churches, and hospitals for the various nationalities. Eventually Galata became too crowded, so that the tide of building moved higher up the slope to the open country of Pera. For centuries, foreigners who wished to visit Stamboul, where the court was installed, could do so only if accompanied by one of the sultan's Janissaries (elite soldiers).

Architecture

Byzantine monuments

Nothing remains of the Byzantium that Constantine chose as the site of New Rome, and almost nothing is left of the mighty city he built there. Constantine's column, the Burnt Column (Çemberlitaş), a shaft of porphyry drums bound by metal laurel leaves, still stands near the Nuruosmaniye mosque complex, but there is no proof that any building in the city dates from his period. Constantine completed the Hippodrome that Septimius Severus had begun, but it was enlarged and rebuilt by his successors until the 5th century. Only its curved end remains, with three columns along the central Spina an obelisk removed from Egypt by the Roman emperor Theodosius I, a masonry obelisk of Constantine VII (Porphyrogenitus; 905–959 CE), and a Delphic column formed by three entwined serpents (now headless) cast after the Battle of Plataea, when the Greeks defeated the Persians in 479 BCE.

Of the myriad columns that decorated Constantinople, there remain standing the base of the column of the emperor Arcadius (reigned 383–408) in the Cerrahpaşa quarter; a column of the emperor Marcian (reigned 450–457), known in Turkish as Kıztaşı (Column of the Virgin), in the Fatih quarter; and, in the grounds of the Topkapı Palace, a perfectly preserved Corinthian column thought to be from the reign of another emperor, Claudius II (Gothicus; 268–270).

Spanning the valley between the third and fourth hills is the two-story limestone aqueduct built in 366 by the emperor Valens. Some of the enormous open-water cisterns of the Byzantine era now serve market gardens. The closed cisterns, of which there are more than 80 remaining, include one of the most beautiful and mysterious structures of Istanbul, the Basilica Cistern, known in Turkish as the Yerebatan Sarayı ("Underground Palace") or Yerebatan Sarnıcı ("Underground Cistern"), near Hagia Sophia; its 336 columns rise from the still, black waters to a vaulted roof.

The Golden Gate is a triumphal arch from about 390. It was built into the defenses of Theodosius II, near the junction of the land and sea walls. The marble-clad bases of its two large towers still stand, and three arches decorated with columns stretch between them.

The only well-preserved example of Byzantine palace architecture is the shell of a three-story rectangular building of limestone and brick, laid in patterns and stripes. Dating from about 1300, it is called the Palace of Constantine (Tekfur Sarayı) and is attached to the land walls not far from the Golden Horn.

The largest legacy from the capital of the vanished empire is 25 Byzantine churches. Many of these are still in use as mosques. The largest of the churches is considered one of the great buildings of the world. This is Hagia Sophia, whose name means "Divine Wisdom." Its contemporary and neighbour, St. Irene, was dedicated to "Divine Peace." Many art historians deem the dome (105 feet [32 metres] in diameter) of Hagia Sophia to be the most beautiful in the world. The church, which shared its clergy with St. Irene, is said to have been built by Constantine in 325 on the foundations of a pagan temple. It was enlarged by the emperor Constans and rebuilt after the fire of 415 by the emperor Theodosius II. The church was burned again in the Nika Insurrection of 532 and reconstructed by Justinian. The structure now standing is essentially the 6th-century edifice, although an earthquake tumbled the dome in 559, after which it was rebuilt to a smaller scale and the whole church reinforced from the outside. It was restored again in the mid-14th century. In 1453 it became a mosque with minarets, and a great chandelier was added. In 1935 it was made into a museum. The walls are still hung with Arabic calligraphic disks.

The Church of Saints Sergius and Bacchus was erected by Justinian between 527 and 536 as a thank-offering. The two soldier-saints allegedly appeared to the emperor Anastasius Ito intercede for Justinian, who had been condemned to death for conspiracy. The church is built as a domed octagon within a rectangle, with a columned and galleried Byzantine interior. It is also called the Mosque of Küçük Ayasofya (Little Sophia) and can be considered an architectural parent of Justinian's reconstruction of Hagia Sophia. The Church of the Holy Saviour in Chora, which was converted into the Kariye Mosque, is near the Adrianople Gate.

It was restored in the 11th century and remodeled in the 14th; the building is now a museum renowned for its 14th-century mosaics, marbles, and frescoes. Over the central portal is a head of Christ with the inscription, "The land of the living." When the church was made a mosque, it acquired the narthex (an enclosed passage between the main entrance and the nave), portico, and minarets.

The Galata district is dominated by a massive tower that shares its name. The tower was built by the Genoese traders in 1349 as a watchtower and a fortification for their walled enclave.

Turkish monuments

When the Turks took possession of Constantinople, they covered the spines of the seven hills with domes and minarets, changing the character of the city. Like the Greeks, the Romans, and the Byzantines, the new rulers loved the city and spent much of their treasure and energy on its embellishment. The Ottoman dynasty, which lasted from 1300 to 1922, continued to build new important structures almost until the end of their line. The most imposing of their mosques were constructed from the mid-15th to the mid-16th century, and the greatest of the architects all bore the name of Sinan.

They were Atik Sinan (the Elder), Sinan of Balıkesir, and Mimar Koca Sinan (Great Architect Sinan). Although the building was deeply influenced by the Persianate traditions of the SeljuqTurks, the style was blended with prevailing Hellenic and Byzantine traditions of the city. Mimar Koca Sinan's masterpiece and his burial place is the Mosque of Süleyman (1550–57), inspired by, but not copied from, Hagia Sophia. It ranks as another of the world's great buildings. Probably the most popularly known of all the mosques in Istanbul is the Blue Mosque, the mosque of Ahmed I (Ottoman sultan from 1603 to 1617), which has six minarets instead of the customary four.

The mosques of the 18th century and later show the effects of importing European architects and craftsmen, who produced Baroque Islamic architecture (such as the Mosque of the Fatih, rebuilt between 1767 and 1771) and even Neoclassical styles, as in the

Dolmabahçe Mosque of 1853, now the Naval Museum. Large mosques were usually built with ancillary structures. Among these were Qur'ānic schools (*medrese*), baths (*hamam*) for purification, hostels and kitchens for the poor (*imaret*), and tombs for royalty and distinguished persons.

There are more than 400 fountains in Istanbul. Some simply flow from wall niches, but others, erected as public philanthropies, are pavilions. The most magnificent of these was built by the sultan Ahmed III in 1728, behind the apse of Hagia Sophia. It is square, with marble walls and bronze gratings, a mixture of the Turkish with the Western Rococo style.

To the north of it, toward the Golden Horn and occupying the whole tip of the promontory, is the sultan's Seraglio (Topkapı Palace), enclosed in a fortified wall. It was begun in 1462 by Mehmed II and served as the residence of the sultans until the beginning of the 19th century. It was to this palace that foreign ambassadors were accredited, and they were admitted through the Imperial Gate, or Bab-ı Hümayun, mistranslated by Westerners as "Sublime Porte." The Seraglio consists mostly of small buildings grouped around three courts.

The most significant buildings are the Çinili Köşk (Tiled Pavilion), built in 1472; the Audience Chamber (Arz Odası); the Hırka-i Şerif, a sanctuary containing relics of the Prophet Muhammad; and the elegant Baghdad Kiosk, commemorating the capture of Baghdad in 1638. The Seraglio houses the sultan's treasure and has important collections of manuscripts, china, armour, and textiles. After the abandonment of the Old Seraglio, the sultans built for themselves palaces along the Bosporus, such as the Beylerbeyi Palace (1865), the lavish Dolmabahçe Palace (1853), the Çırağan Palace (built in 1874 and burned in 1910), and the Yıldız Palace, which was the residence of Abdülhamid II, Ottoman sultan from 1876 to 1909.

The Grand Bazaar (Kapalı Çarşı), founded early in the Turkish regime but often subject to fire and earthquake, had 4,000 shops around two central distributing houses. The district is laid out on a grid plan. It still bustles with life and the pursuit of piastres.

The L-shaped Egyptian Bazaar (Mısır Çarşısı) so called because it is adjacent to the Yeni Valide Mosque complex, the construction of which was financed by taxes from Cairo was once a dedicated spice market. In later times the shops expanded their wares to include dried fruit, jewelry, linens, and other goods.

History

Earliest times

Semistra, the earliest-known settlement on the site of İstanbul, was probably founded around 1000 BC, a few hundred years after the Trojan War and in the same period that kings David and Solomon ruled in Jerusalem. Semistra was followed by a fishing village named Lygos, which occupied Seraglio Point (Seray Burnu) where Topkapı Palace stands today.

Around 700 BC, colonists from Megara (near Corinth) in Greece founded the city of Chalcedon (now Kadıköy) on the Asian shore of the Bosphorus. Chalcedon became one of a dozen Greek fishing colonies along the shores of the Propontis (the ancient name for the

Sea of Marmara). The historian Theopompus of Chios, cited in John Freely's *Istanbul: The Imperial City,* wrote in the latter half of the 4th century that its inhabitants 'devoted themselves unceasingly to the better pursuits of life'. Their way of life was apparently in stark contrast to that of the dissolute Byzantines, who founded their settlement across the Bosphorus at Seraglio Point in 657 BC.

First incarnation: Byzantium

Legend tells us that Byzantium was founded by a Megarian colonist named Byzas, the son of the god Poseidon and the nymph Keroessa, daughter of Zeus and Io. Before leaving Greece, Byzas had asked the oracle at Delphi where he should establish his new colony. The enigmatic answer was 'Opposite the blind'. All this made sense when Byzas and his fellow colonists sailed up the Bosphorus and noticed the colony on the Asian shore at Chalcedon. Looking west, they saw the small fishing village of Lygos, built on a magnificent and easily fortified natural harbour of the Golden Horn (known to the Greeks as Chrysokeras) on the European shore. Thinking, as legend has it, that the settlers of Chalcedon must have been blind to disregard such a superb position, Byzas and his mates settled here and their new town came to be called Byzantium after its founder.

The new colony quickly prospered, largely due to its ability to levy tolls and harbour fees on ships passing through the Bosphorus, then as now an important waterway. A thriving marketplace was established and the inhabitants lived on traded goods and the abundant fish stocks in the surrounding waters. In all, the early Byzantines were a fortunate lot. They walled their city to ensure its invincibility from attack, enslaved the local Thracian population to do most of the hard work and worshipped the Greek Olympian gods. Theopompus of Chios might have thought that the Chalcedons lived a good clean life when they first established their city on the opposite shore, but he had no such compliment for the Byzantines, writing that they 'accustomed themselves to amours and drinking in the taverns'.

In 512 BC Darius, emperor of Persia, captured the city during his campaign against the Scythians. Following the retreat of the Persians in 478 BC, the town came under the influence and protection of Athens and joined the Athenian League. It was a turbulent relationship, with Byzantium revolting a number of times, only to be defeated by the Athenians. During one of the revolts, the Athenian navy mounted an expedition against Byzantium and Chalcedon and sailed up the Bosphorus to establish a settlement at Chrysopolis ('the City of Gold'), site of the present-day suburb of Üsküdar. From this base they successfully besieged Byzantium.

The Spartans took the city after the end of the Peloponnesian War (404 BC) but were ousted in 390 BC, when Byzantium once again joined the League of Athens. It was granted independence in 355 BC but stayed under the Athenian umbrella, withstanding with

Athenian help a siege by Philip, father of Alexander the Great, in 340 BC.

By the end of the Hellenistic period, Byzantium had formed an alliance with the Roman Empire. It retained its status as a free state, which it even kept after being officially incorporated into the Roman Empire in AD 79 by Vespasian, but it paid significant taxes for the privilege. Life was relatively uneventful until the city's leaders made a big mistake: they picked the wrong side in a Roman war of succession following the death of the Emperor Pertinax in AD 193. When Septimius Severus emerged victorious over his rival Pescennius Niger, he mounted a three-year siege of the city, eventually massacring Byzantium's citizens, razing its walls and burning it to the ground. Ancient Byzantium was no more.

The new emperor was aware of the city's important strategic position, and he soon set about rebuilding it. He pardoned the remaining citizens and built a circuit of walls that stretched roughly from where the Yeni

Camii is today to the Bucoleon Palace, enclosing a city twice the size of its predecessor. The Hippodrome was built by Severus, as was a colonnaded way that followed the present path of Divan Yolu. He also erected a gateway known as the Miliarium Aureum or, more simply, the Milion. A marble stellae from this gate can still be seen today. Severus named his new city Augusta Antonina and it was subsequently ruled by a succession of emperors, including the great Diocletian (r 284–303).

Decline of Rome & the rise of Constantinople

Diocletian had decreed that after his retirement, the government of the Roman Empire should be overseen by co-emperors Galerius in the east (Augusta Antonina) and Constantine in the west (Rome). This resulted in a civil war, which was won by Constantine in AD 324 when he defeated Licinius, Galerius' successor, at Chrysopolis.

With his victory, Constantine became sole emperor (r 324–37) of a reunited empire. He also became the first Christian emperor, though he didn't formally convert until on his deathbed. To solidify his power he summoned the First Ecumenical Council at Nicaea (İznik) in 325, which established the precedent of the emperor's supremacy in church affairs.

Constantine also decided to move the capital of the empire to the shores of the Bosphorus. He built a new, wider circle of walls around the site of Byzantium and laid out a magnificent city within. The Hippodrome was extended and a forum was built on the crest of the second hill, near today's Nuruosmaniye Camii. The city was dedicated on 11 May 330 as New Rome, but soon came to be called Constantinople. First settled as a fishing village over 1000 years earlier, the settlement on Seraglio Point was now the capital of the Eurasian world and would remain so for almost another 1000 years.

Constantine died in 337, just seven years after the dedication of his new capital. His empire was divided up between his three sons: Constantius, Constantien and Constans. Constantinople was part of Constantius' share. His power base was greatly increased in 353 when he overthrew both of his brothers and brought the empire under his sole control.

Constantius died in 361 and was succeeded by his cousin Julian. Emperor Jovian was next, succeeded by Valens (of aqueduct fame).

The city continued to grow under the rule of the emperors. Theodosius I ('the Great') had a forum built on the present site of Beyazıt Square and a massive triumphal gate built in the city walls, the Porta Aurea (Golden Gate). He also erected the Obelisk of Theodosius at the Hippodrome. His grandson Emperor Theodosius II (r 408–50) came to the throne as a boy, heavily influenced by his sister Pulcheria, who acted as regent until her brother was old enough to rule in his own right.

Threatened by the forces of Attila the Hun, he ordered that an even wider, more formidable circle of walls be built around the city. Encircling all seven hills of the city, the walls were completed in 413, only to be brought down by a series of earthquakes in 447. They were hastily rebuilt in a mere two months the rapid approach of Attila and the Huns acting as a powerful stimulus. The Theodosian walls successfully held out invaders for the next 757 years and still stand today, though they are in an increasingly dilapidated state of repair.

Theodosius II's other achievements were the compilation of the *Codex Theodosianus,* a collection of all of the laws that had been enacted since the reign of Constantine the Great, and the erection of a new cathedral, the Sancta Sophia (Aya Sofya), which replaced an earlier church of the same name that had been burned down during a riot in 404.

Justinian & Theodora

Theodosius died in 450 and was succeeded by a string of emperors, including the most famous of all Byzantine emperors, Justinian.

During the 5th and 6th centuries, as the barbarians of Europe captured and sacked Rome, the new eastern capital grew in wealth, strength and reputation. Justinian (r 527–65) had much to do with this. A former soldier, he and his great general Belisarius reconquered Anatolia, the Balkans, Egypt, Italy and North Africa. They also successfully put down the Nika riots of 532, killing 30, 000 of the rioters in the Hippodrome in the process.

Three years before taking the throne, Justinian had married Theodora, a strong-willed former courtesan who is credited with having great influence over her husband. Together, they further embellished Constantinople with great buildings, including SS Sergius and Bacchus, now known as Küçük Aya Sofya, Hagia Eirene (Aya İrini) and the Basilica Cistern.

Justinian's personal triumph was the new Sancta Sophia (Aya Sofya), which was completed in 537.

Justinian's ambitious building projects and constant wars of reconquest exhausted his treasury and his empire. Following his reign, the Byzantine Empire would never again be as large, powerful or rich.

Under siege & in decline

From 565 to 1025, a succession of warrior emperors kept invaders such as the Persians and the Avars at bay. Though the foreign armies often managed to get as far as Chalcedon, none were able to breach Theodosius' great walls. The Arab armies of the nascent Islamic empire tried in 669, 674, 678 and 717–18, each time in vain. Inside the walls the city was undergoing a different type of threat: the Iconoclastic Crisis. This began in 726 when Emperor Leo III launched his quest to rid the empire of all forms of idolatry. Those who worshipped idols, including the followers of many saints, revolted and a number of uprisings ensued. The emperor was ultimately triumphant and his policy was adopted by his successors. It was first overturned in 780, when the Empress Eirene, mother of the child emperor Constantine VI, set out to restore icons. The issue was finally put to rest by the Empress Theodora, mother of Michael III, another child emperor, in 845.

The powerful emperors of the Bulgarian empire besieged the city in 814, 913 and 924, never conquering it. Under Emperor Basil II (r 976–1025), the Byzantine armies drove the Arab armies out of Anatolia and completely annihilated the Bulgarian forces. For this feat he was dubbed Bulgaroctonus, the 'Bulgar-slayer'.

In 1071 Emperor Romanus IV Diogenes (r 1068–1071) led his army to eastern Anatolia to do battle with the Seljuk Turks, who had been forced out of Central Asia by the encroaching Mongols. However, at Manzikert (Malazgirt) the Byzantines were disastrously defeated, the emperor captured and imprisoned, and the former

Byzantine heartland of Anatolia thus thrown open to Turkish invasion and settlement. Soon the Seljuks had built a thriving empire of their own in central Anatolia, with their capital first at Nicaea and later at Konya.

As Turkish power was consolidated in Anatolia to the east of Constantinople, the power of Venice always a maritime and commercial rival to Constantinople grew in the west. This coincided with the launch of the First Crusade and the arrival in Constantinople of the first of the Crusaders in 1096.

The Crusaders: interlopers from the West

Soldiers of the Second Crusade passed through the city in 1146 during the reign of Manuel I, son of John Comnenus II 'The Good' and his empress, Eirene, both of whose mosaic portraits can be seen in the gallery at Aya Sofya. In 1171 Manuel evicted Venetian merchants from their neighbourhood in Galata. The Venetians retaliated by sending a fleet to attack Byzantine ports in Greece.

The convoluted, treacherous imperial court politics of Constantinople have given us the word 'Byzantine'. Rarely blessed with a simple, peaceful succession, Byzantine rulers were always under threat from members of their own families as well as would-be tyrants and foreign powers. This internecine plotting was eventually to lead to the defeat of the city by the Crusaders.

In 1195 Alexius III deposed and blinded his brother, Emperor Isaac II, claiming the throne for himself. Fleeing to the West, Isaac's oldest son, Prince Alexius, pleaded to the Pope and other Western rulers for help in restoring his father to the Byzantine throne. At the time, the Fourth Crusade was assembling in Venice to sail to Egypt and attack the infidel. Knowing this, Prince Alexius sent a message to the Crusaders offering to agree to a union of the Greek and Roman churches under the papacy if the Crusaders could put his father back on the throne. He also promised to pay richly for their assistance. The Crusader leaders agreed, and Enrico Dandolo, Doge of Venice, led the crusaders to Constantinople, arriving in 1203.

Rather than facing the Crusaders, Alexius III fled with the imperial treasury. The Byzantines swiftly restored Isaac II to the throne and made Prince Alexius his co-emperor. Unfortunately, the new co-emperors had no money to pay their allies. They were also deeply unpopular with their subjects, being seen as Latin toadies. Isaac fell ill (he died in 1204), and the Byzantines swiftly deposed Alexius and crowned a new emperor, Alexius V. The new emperor foolishly ordered the Crusaders to leave his territory, conveniently ignoring the fact that they believed themselves to be owed a considerable amount of money by the Byzantines. Their patience exhausted, the Crusaders attacked. On 13 April 1204 they broke through the walls, and sacked and pillaged the rich capital of their Christian ally.

When the smoke cleared, Dandolo took control of three-eighths of the city, including Aya Sofya, leaving the rest to his co-conspirator Count Baldwin of Flanders. The Byzantine nobility fled to what was left of their estates and fought among themselves in best Byzantine fashion for control of the shreds of the empire.

After Dandolo's death, Count Baldwin had himself crowned emperor of Romania('Kingdom of the Romans'), his name for his new kingdom. Never a strong or effective state, Baldwin's so-called empire steadily declined until, just over half a century later in 1261, it was easily recaptured by the soldiers of Michael VIII Palaeologus, formerly the emperor of Nicaea, where the Byzantine Empire in exile sat. The Byzantine Empire was restored.

The Ottomans: upstarts from the East

Two decades after Michael reclaimed Constantinople, a Turkish warlord named Ertuğrul died in the village of Söğüt near Nicaea. He left his son Osman, who was known as Gazi (Warrior for the Faith), a small territory. Osman's followers became known in the Empire as Osmanlıs and in the West as the Ottomans.

Osman died in 1324 and was succeeded by his son Orhan. In 1326 Orhan captured Bursa, made it his capital and took the title of sultan. A victory at Nicaea followed, after which he sent his forces further afield, conquering Ankara to the east and Thrace to the west. His son Murat I (r 1362–89) took Adrianople (Edirne) in 1371 and extended his conquests to Kosovo, where he defeated the Serbs and Bosnians.

Murat's son Beyazıt (r 1389–1402) unsuccessfully laid siege to Constantinople in 1394, then defeated a Crusader army 100,000 strong on the Danube in 1396. Though temporarily checked by the armies of Tamerlane and a nasty war of succession between Beyazıt's four sons that was eventually won by

Mehmet I (r 1413–21), the Ottomans continued to grow in power and size. By 1440 the Ottoman armies under Murat II (r 1421–51) had taken Thessalonica, unsuccessfully laid siege to Constantinople and Belgrade, and battled Christian armies for Transylvania. It was at this point in history that Mehmet II 'The Conqueror' (r 1451–81) came to power and vowed to attain the ultimate prize Constantinople.

The conquest

By 1450, the Byzantine emperor had control over little more than Constantinople itself.

The first step in Mehmet's plan to take the city was construction of the great fortress of Rumeli Hisarı, which was completed in 1452. He also repaired Anadolu Hisarı, the fortress on the Asian shore that had been built by his great-grandfather. Between them, the two great fortresses then closed the Bosphorus at its narrowest point, blockading the imperial capital from the north.

The Byzantines had closed the mouth of the Golden Horn with a heavy chain (on view in İstanbul's Askeri Müzesi) to prevent Ottoman ships from sailing in and attacking the city walls on the north side. Mehmet outsmarted them by marshalling his boats at a cove where Dolmabahçe Palace now stands, and having them transported overland during the night on rollers and slides up the valley (where the İstanbul Hilton now stands) and down the other side into the Golden Horn at Kasımpaşa. As dawn broke his fleet attacked the city, catching the Byzantine defenders by surprise. Soon the Golden Horn was under Ottoman control.

As for the mighty Theodosian land walls to the west, a Hungarian cannon founder named Urban had offered his services to the Byzantine emperor for the defence of Christendom. Finding that the emperor had no money, he conveniently forgot about defending Christianity and went instead to Mehmet, who paid him richly to cast an enormous cannon capable of firing a huge ball right through the city walls.

Despite the inevitability of the conquest (Mehmet had 80,000 men compared with Byzantium's 7000), Emperor Constantine XI (r 1449–53) refused the surrender terms offered by Mehmet on 23 May 1453, preferring to wait in hope that Christendom would come to his rescue. On 28 May the final attack commenced: the mighty walls were breached between the gates now called Topkapı and Edirnekapı, the sultan's troops flooded in and by the evening of the 29th they were in control of every quarter. Constantine, the last emperor of Byzantium, died fighting on the city walls.

The city ascendant

The 21-year-old conqueror saw himself as the successor to the imperial throne of Byzantium by right of conquest, and he began to rebuild and repopulate the city. Aya Sofya was converted to a mosque; a new mosque, the Fatih (Conqueror) Camii, was built on the fourth hill; and the Eski Saray (Old Palace) was constructed on the third hill, followed by a new palace at Topkapı a few years later. The city walls were repaired and a new fortress, Yedikule, was built. İstanbul, as it was often called, became the new administrative, commercial and cultural centre of the ever-growing Ottoman Empire. Mehmet encouraged Greeks who had fled the city to return and issued an imperial decree calling for resettlement; Muslims, Jews and Christians all took up his offer and were promised the right to worship as they pleased. The Genoese, who had fought with the Byzantines, were pardoned and allowed to stay in Galata, though the fortifications that surrounded their settlement were torn down. Only Galata Tower was allowed to stand.

Mehmet died in 1481 and was succeeded by Beyazıt II (r 1481–1512), who was ousted by his son, the ruthless Selim the Grim (r 1512–20), famed for executing seven grand viziers and numerous relatives during his relatively short reign.

The building boom that Mehmet kicked off was continued by his successors, with Selim's son Süleyman the Magnificent (r 1520–66) being responsible for more construction than any other sultan. Blessed with the services of Mimar Sinan (1497–1588), Islam's greatest architect, the sultan and his family, court and grand viziers crowded the city with great buildings. Under Süleyman's 46-year reign, the longest of any sultan, the empire expanded its territories and refined its artistic pursuits at its court. None of the empires of Europe or Asia were as powerful.

Rule of the women

Süleyman's son Selim II ('the Sot', r 1566–74) and his successors lost themselves in the pleasures of the harem and the bottle, and cared little for the administration of the empire their forebears had built. While they were carousing, a succession of exceptionally able grand viziers dealt with external and military affairs.

Before the drunken Selim drowned in his bath, his chief concubine Nurbanu called the shots in the palace and ushered in the so-called 'Rule of the Women', whereby a series of chief concubines and mothers (*valide sultans*) of a series of dissolute sultans ruled the roost at court. Among the most fascinating of these women was Kösem Sultan, the favourite of Sultan Ahmet I (r 1603–17). She influenced the course of the empire through Ahmet, then through her sons Murat IV (r 1623–40) and İbrahim, ('the Mad', r 1640–48) and finally through her grandson Mehmet IV (r 1648–87). Her influence over Mehmet lasted only a few years and she was strangled in 1651 at the command of the *valide sultan* Turhan Hadice, Mehmet's mother.

For the next century the sultans continued in Selim's footsteps. Their dissolute and often unbalanced behaviour led to dissatisfaction among the people and the army, which would eventually prove to be the empire's undoing.

Decline, then attempts at reform

The motor that drove the Ottoman Empire was military conquest, and when the sultan's armies reached their geographical and technological limits, decline set in for good. In 1683 the Ottomans laid siege for the second time to Vienna, but failed again to take the city. With the Treaty of Karlowitz in 1699, the Austrian and Ottoman emperors divided up the Balkans, and the Ottoman Empire went on the defensive.

By this time Europe was well ahead of Turkey in politics, technology, science, banking, commerce and military development. Sultan Selim III (r 1789–1807) initiated efforts to catch up to Europe, but was overthrown in a revolt by janissaries (the sultan's personal bodyguards). The modernisation efforts were continued under Mahmut II (r 1808–39). He founded a new army along European lines, provoking a riot among the janissaries, so that in 1826 he had to send his new force in to crush them, which it did. The bodies of janissaries filled the Hippodrome and the ancient corps, once the glory of the empire, was no more.

Sultan Abdül Mecit (r 1839–61) continued the catch-up, continuing the Tanzimat (Reorganisation) political and social reforms that had been initiated by his father Mahmut II. But these efforts were too little, too late. During the 19th century, ethnic nationalism, a force more powerful even than Western armies, penetrated the empire's domain and proved its undoing.

Ethnic nationalism

For centuries, the non-Turkish ethnic and non-Muslim religious minorities in the sultan's domains had lived side by side with their Turkish neighbours, governed by their own religious and traditional laws. The head of each community chief rabbi, Orthodox patriarch etc was responsible to the sultan for the community's wellbeing and behaviour.

Ottoman decline and misrule provided fertile ground for the growth of ethnic nationalism among these communities. The subject peoples of the Ottoman Empire rose in revolt, one after another, often with the direct encouragement and assistance of the European powers, who coveted parts of the sultan's vast domains. After bitter fighting in 1831 the Kingdom of Greece was formed; the Serbs, Bulgarians, Romanians, Albanians, Armenians and Arabs would all seek their independence soon after.

As the sultan's empire broke up, the European powers (Britain, France, Italy, Germanyand Russia) hovered in readiness to colonise or annex the pieces. They used religion as a reason for pressure or control, saying that it was their duty to protect the sultan's Catholic, Protestant or Orthodox subjects from misrule and anarchy.

The Russian emperors put pressure on the Turks to grant them powers over all Ottoman Orthodox Christian subjects, whom the Russian emperor would thus 'protect'. The result was the Crimean War (1853–56), with Britain and France fighting on the side of the

Ottomans against the growth of Russian power. During the war, wounded British, French and Ottoman soldiers were brought to İstanbul for treatment at the Selimiye Army Barracks, now home to the Florence Nightingale Museum, and the foundations of modern nursing practice were laid.

Even during the war, the sultan continued the imperial building tradition. Vast Dolmabahçe Palace and its mosque were finished in 1856, and the palaces at Beylerbeyi, Çırağan and Yıldız would be built before the end of the century. Though it had lost the fabulous wealth of the days of Süleyman the Magnificent, the city was still regarded as the Paris of the East. It was also the terminus of the *Orient Express,* which connected İstanbul and Paris the world's first great international luxury express train.

Abdül Hamit II & the young Turks

Amid the empire's internal turmoil, Abdül Hamit II (r 1876–1909) assumed the throne. Mithat Paşa, a successful general and powerful grand vizier, managed to introduce a constitution at the same time, but soon the new sultan did away both with Mithat Paşa and the constitution, and established his own absolute rule.

Abdül Hamit modernised without democratising, building thousands of kilometres of railways and telegraph lines and encouraging modern industry. However, the empire continued to disintegrate, and there were nationalist insurrections in Armenia, Bulgaria, Crete and Macedonia.

The younger generation of the Turkish elite particularly the military watched bitterly as their country fell apart, then organised secret societies bent on toppling the sultan. The Young Turk movement for Western-style reforms gained enough power by 1908 to force the restoration of the constitution. In 1909 the Young Turk-led Ottoman parliament deposed Abdül Hamit and put his hopelessly indecisive brother Mehmet V on the throne.

When WWI broke out, the Ottoman parliament and sultan made the fatal error of siding with Germany and the Central Powers. With their defeat, the Ottoman Empire collapsed, İstanbul was occupied by the British and the sultan became a pawn in the hands of the victors.

Republican Istanbul

The situation looked very bleak for the Turks as their armies were being disbanded and their country was taken under the control of the Allies, but what first seemed a catastrophe provided the impetus for rebirth.

Since gaining independence in 1831, the Greeks had entertained the Megali Idea (Great Plan) of a new Greek empire encompassing all the lands that had once had Greek influence in effect, the refounding of the Byzantine Empire, with Constantinople as its capital. On 15 May 1919, with Western backing, Greek armies invaded Anatolia in order to make the dream a reality.

Even before the Greek invasion an Ottoman general named Mustafa Kemal, the hero of the WWI battle at Gallipoli, had decided that a new government must take over the destiny of the Turks from the ineffectual sultan. He began organising resistance to the sultan's captive government on 19 May 1919.

The Turkish War of Independence, in which the Turkish Nationalist forces led by Mustafa Kemal fought off Greek, French and Italian invasion forces, lasted from 1920 to 1922. Victory in the bitter war put Mustafa Kemal (1881–1938) in command of the fate of the Turks. The sultanate was abolished in 1922, as was the Ottoman Empire soon after. The republic was born on 29 October 1923.

Downgraded: no longer the capital

The nation's saviour, proclaimed Atatürk (Father Turk) by the Turkish parliament, decided to move away, both metaphorically and physically, from the imperial memories of İstanbul. He established the seat of the new republican government in a city (Ankara) that could not be threatened by foreign gunboats. Robbed of its importance as the capital of a vast empire, İstanbul lost much of its wealth and glitter in succeeding decades.

Atatürk had always been ill at ease with Islamic traditions and he set about making the Republic of Turkey a secular state. The fez (Turkish brimless cap) was abolished, as was polygamy; Friday was replaced by Sunday as the day of rest; surnames were introduced; the Arabic alphabet was replaced by a Latin script; and civil (not religious) marriage became mandatory. The country's modernisation was accompanied by a great surge of nationalistic pride, and though it was no longer the political capital, İstanbul continued to be the centre of the nation's cultural and economic life.

Atatürk died in İstanbul in 1938, just before WWII broke out, and was succeeded as president by Ismet İnönü. Still scarred from the calamity of its involvement in the Great War, Turkey managed to successfully stay out of the new conflict until 1945, when it entered on the Allied side.

The coup years

The Allies made it clear that they believed that Turkey should introduce democracy. The government agreed and called parliamentary elections. The first opposition party in Turkey's history the Democratic Party led by Adnan Menderes won the first of these elections in 1950.

Though he started as a democrat, Menderes became increasingly autocratic. In 1960 the military staged a coup against his government and convicted him and two of his ministers of treason. All three were hanged in 1961. New elections were held and a government was formed, but it and ensuing administrations were dogged by corruption charges, and constitutional violations and amendments. In 1971 the military staged another coup, only to repeat the process in

1980 and install a military junta, which ruled for three years before new elections were called. It seemed to many observers that the far left and extreme right factions in the country would never be able to reconcile, and that military coups would be a constant feature of the modern political landscape. However, voters in the 1983 election refused to see this as a *fait accompli* and, rather than voting in the military's preferred candidates, elected the reforming Motherland party of economist Turgut Özal. A new era had begun.

The recent past

Under the presidency of economist Turgut Özal, the 1980s saw a free market-led economic and tourism boom in Turkey and its major city. Özal's government also presided over a great increase in urbanisation, with trainloads of peasants from eastern Anatolia making their way to the cities particularly İstanbul in search of jobs in the booming industry sector. The city's infrastructure couldn't cope back then and is still catching up, despite nearly three decades of large-scale municipal works being undertaken.

The municipal elections of March 1994 were a shock to the political establishment, with the upstart religious-right Refah Partisi (Welfare Party) winning elections across the country. Its victory was seen in part as a protest vote against the corruption, ineffective policies and tedious political wrangles of the traditional parties. In İstanbul Refah was led by Recep Tayyip Erdoğan, a proudly Islamist candidate. He vowed to modernise infrastructure and restore the city to its former glory.

In the national elections of December 1996, Refah polled more votes than any other party (23%), and eventually formed a government vowing moderation and honesty. Emboldened by political power, Prime Minister Necmettin Erbakan and other Refah politicians tested the boundaries of Turkey's traditional secularism, alarming the powerful National Security Council, the most visible symbol of the centrist military establishment's role as the caretaker of secularism and democracy.

In 1997 the council announced that Refah had flouted the constitutional ban on religion in politics and warned that the government should resign or face a military coup. Bowing to the inevitable, Erbakan did as the council wished. In İstanbul, Mayor Erdoğan was ousted by the secularist forces in the national government in late 1998.

National elections in April 1999 brought in a coalition government led by Bülent Ecevit's left-wing Democratic Left Party. After years under the conservative right of the Refah Partisi, the election result heralded a shift towards European-style social democracy, something highlighted by the country's successful bid to be accepted as a candidate for membership of the European Union. Unfortunately for the new government there was a spectacular collapse of the Turkish economy in 2001, leading to an electoral defeat in 2002. The victorious party was the moderate

Islamic Justice and Development Party, led by Phoenix-like Recep Tayyip Erdoğan who despite continuing tensions with military hardliners has run an increasingly stable and prosperous Turkey ever since.

Cultural Life

The Atatürk Cultural Center, situated in Taksim Square, is an important centre for the arts where opera, ballet, and theatre performances are staged. The municipal theatre operates several playhouses, and there are many theatre companies.

A large number of learned societies and research institutes are headquartered in the city, including the Turkish Law Association (Türk Hukuk Kurumu), Turkish Historical Society (Türk Tarih Kurumu), German and French archaeological institutes, and the Turkish Language Institute (Türk Dil Kurumu). There is a nuclear research centre at Küçükçekmece.

There are many public and private libraries. The small, specialized Köprülü Library (1677) has books from early Ottoman presses and handwritten works more than 1,000 years old. Many of the city's mosques, palaces, and monuments, as mentioned earlier, contain museums. Other museums include the Archaeological Museums of Istanbul (İstanbul Arkeoloji Müzeleri), the Museum of Turkish and Islamic Art (Türk ve İslam Eserleri Müzesi), and the Military Museum and Cultural Center (Askeri Müze ve Kültür Sitesi Komutanlığı).

The Hippodrome is now a public garden; there are also numerous other public parks. A unique feature of the city is its market gardens, which are associated with the open cisterns that formed early Constantinople's water-supply system. The cisterns have been partially built over and are called Çukur Bostan (Hollow Gardens).

Football (soccer) is a popular sport, and Istanbul has a number of stadiums, including BJK İnönü, Vefa, Fenerbahçe Şükrü Saracoğlu, Atatürk Olympic stadium, and Türk Telekom Arena. Florya and Ataköy are popular beaches on the Sea of Marmara.

Travel and Tourism

ISTANBUL TRAVEL GUIDE

Istanbul is hustling, beautiful, busy, chaotic, romantic, historic, kitsch, gorgeous depending on which part of the city you are and the time of day. A city of over 14 million people the time of day really would change the impression you get from where you are at. People move in this vast city built on two continents crossing continents, covering huge distances within the city. You may still relax, take your time and enjoy as long as you go to the right places at the right times. Want to relax? Then hit a side street, take a boat cruise, sit at a cafe on the Bosphorus, immerse yourself in Byzantine times in the quiet of a mosaic museum or watch the beautiful tiles in Blue Mosque. Want to see some city rush and human touch? Then go to Istiklal Street and just watch people pass by.

European side is the business side, Asian the residential. Most people who work at foreign and domestic major corporations have left the city center for a life in the far suburbs where big gated communities, or even small scale cities in peripheries of Istanbul and are commuting daily to the city center. But they sure are missing the center!

Where ever you go, one thing is for sure: there's something strange about this city. May be it is because it has seen three empires in its long history: East Roman, Byzantine and Ottoman Empires. May be it has seen so many kinds of people from different parts of the world: Europe, Middle East, Central Asia, Eurasia, Africa.. Or may be it is just this strange mix that it offers. A blend of east and west or a fusion of old and new or a combination of traditional and modern. Is Istanbul the furthest east of the west? Or is it just the other way around? Are Turks eastern or western? Is "contrast" an Istanbul born phenomenon?

You have to see it yourself and decide. The Vikings named it Miklagard "big city", the Slavs called it Tsarigrad, "City of Caesar", for the Greeks it has been Konstantinapolis. May be you will have a name of your own for Istanbul once you get to see this place. The thing is: you have to see this place.

Traveling to Istanbul Guide
Coming in to Istambul

Visa requirements
You probably need a visa to enter Turkey, which can usually be obtained online. Check if this applies to you, and apply in advance, at evisa.gov.tr. Do not rely upon any other site, even here at Wikitravel, as the rules may change suddenly as the security situation in Turkey evolves. Also some sites charge extra for no additional service. In general EU Schengen passport holders need a visa to enter, North American and UK

residents need a visa costing US$ 20 valid for 90 days, residents of China pay US$ 60 for 30 days, and visa duration and price varies for other nations. Some travelers are not eligible for an evisa and must apply for a conventional visa via their local Turkish Embassy. However these same travelers who are otherwise ineligible with solely their citizenship may be eligible for an eVisa if they hold a valid visa or residence permit for Schengen, USA, UK or Ireland. For example Indian citizens are eligible for a single entry Turkish eVisa if they hold a valid visa or residence permit for Schengen, USA, UK or Ireland. Indian citizens have to pay a fee of US$ 43 for an eVisa provided they meet that criteria. However you should always go directly to official sites to check visa requirements and it is recommended you visit Government of Turkey e-Visa site to learn more about Turkish eVisas.

Apply at the same time as you book your trip - your 90 (or other) day visa validity will start from your stated arrival day in Turkey. Print it out and keep it with you, as well as a soft copy on your phone. As well as checks when flying, it could be demanded at an internal police check.

In theory you are permitted to arrive at Ataturk airport without a visa and use the visa office or machine to apply there (Visa on arrival). However this is only available for certain nationalities.

Coming by plane

Atatürk Airport

Most planes arrive at Istanbul Atatürk Airport (IATA: IST), 20km west of the city centre. From the airport, there are various options for getting into Istanbul: you can take a taxi (about TRY60 to Taksim. There is no night fare in Istanbul anymore - the price would be the same at midnight or midday. About the same to Sultanahmet), the express bus service run by the local airport service called "Havataş" [29] which departs half-hourly between 4AM-midnight and costs TRY11 (July 2016) to Taksim and Aksaray, the public bus (line #96T) run by *İETT* costing TRY5 (TRY3.50 with

İstanbulKart), which has fewer departure times now, due to Havatas, which is also a municipality engaged bus service. At the bus stop of your final destination, be wary of taxi drivers that come up to you or are overly friendly. Follow locals to a corner where most of the taxis are picking up customers.

Then, there is the metro (06:00-00:05) (signposted "light rail" in the airport, when you get outside the baggage claim it's about a 10 minute walk in the airport to the metro line. Just follow the signs), which will take you directly to the *Otogar* (bus station) or to numerous stops within Istanbul (Aksaray in the city centre is the last stop, transfer stations for tram heading for deeper into old city is available at Zeytinburnu and Aksaray). It costs TRY3, by token (+an extra TRY4 when boarding the tram) and getting to Aksaray takes around 45 minutes. It is possible to be at your bus departing from *Otogar* within less than one hour after landing by taking the metro. (Actual travel time on the metro from the Aksaray station to the

Airport station was 35 minutes and cost TL 2.60 with the Istanbulkart, June 2018. Obviously allow more time if you need to transfer on the way to the airport and keep in mind that you will have to pay for the transfer.)

When entering the metro station, you need to buy a *jeton* (token) for TRY4. Just hand the cashier TRY4 and he'll give you a token, or use the automatic dispenser (*Jetonmatik*), which accepts banknotes (TRY5, TRY10, TRY20) as well as coins. Use 'select' to choose the number of jetons and then push 'ok'. They don't accept credit card or foreign currency here. This will get you on the red metro line (towards Aksaray). From this line, if you are going to Sultanahmet, you can transfer at Zeytinburnu and buy another *jeton* (TRY4) - see the section on "Istanbulkart" if further travel within Istanbul's metro system will be undertaken. Note that the *jeton* token here is different than the first one. From Zeytinburnu, take the blue tram line T1, towards Kabataşwhich passes by: Sultanahmet, Eminönu and

Tophane. The trip from the airport to Sultanahmet takes about 45min.

To get from Ataturk to the Asian side of Istanbul, the quickest way is to take a taxi to Bakikoy IDO Iskele (ferry pier), which takes about 10m and costs 20TL, and then take an IDO high-speed catamaran to Kadikoy (20m) or Bostanci (40m) for 7TL. This is much faster and cheaper than a taxi, which could take up to 2 hours if there is a lot of traffic. The boat runs from 7am to 9pm.

Other Notes: Note that people are working on commission at the airport trying to make you use special shuttle buses for very high fees (TRY30+), so for people who wish to travel more economically the Metro/tram-combination is easy and fairly quick, and offers very good value. Travel by metro/tram cost 1 token per trip which is equal to TRY3. No matter how long you travel, it costs 1 token per trip.

Food and drink at the airport may cost up to five times more than in the city proper, like in other international airports. If you are travelling on budget and plan to spend some time at the airport, it may be wise to bring your own meals from town instead of buying them there. If you come from the Metro, there is a supermarket in the tunnel leading to the elevators / stairs to the airport proper where you can do some last-minute shopping.

Sabiha Gökçen Airport
Istanbul also has a second airport, Sabiha Gökçen International Airport (IATA: SAW), located in the Anatolian side of the city Sabiha Gökçen International Airport.

The cheapest way to arrive from Sabiha Gökçen to the European side of Istanbul is by bus (E10 or E11 lines, from Sabiha Gökçen to Kadiköy) + ferry (from Kadiköy to many ferry stations, including some in the Sultanahmet area). Using Istanbulkart or Akbil (see below), the price is less than TRY7. That's about €2.50

in total. Every other option priced at €10 and above (TRY23 and above-by Feb 2013 rates) makes sense ONLY if you can't use this. Be aware that last ferries are between 10 and 11pm, yet the E10 continues throughout the night.

A pricier option is the *Havatas* bus connects this airport with Taksim in the city centre for TRY14 (Aug 2014) and takes about an hour and a half (closer to two or more in heavy traffic). There is also a Havatas service to the ferry pier in Kadıköy, a transportation hub of Asian Side, which costs TRY 10. If you arrive in the middle of the night, you can move to the departure hall after passing customs and rest on very comfortable seats you will even find coin-operated Japanese massage chairs. Then, at 05:00 the first Havatas bus will take you to town. The Havatas bus schedule is sometimes linked to the arrival/departure times of planes.

Various private operators offer internet bookable shared minibuses to central locations a good choice when arriving late. A typical price being €90 for 4 people to a hotel in Laleli. A taxi to Sabiha Gökçen airport from Taksim, which lies around 50km from the airport, takes c. 35 minutes at 03:30 with no traffic. The meter will show c. TRY75, plus there is c. TRY6 in tolls. Note the security screening is *before* the check-in counters, so add some extra time to make the cut-off times (45 minutes for international, 30 for domestic).

Beware of the company running the "Hotel Information" office in the Sabiha Gökçen airport which offers "shuttle-to-hotel" services from €15 (they pretend to make a discount based on your group size, you can get it as low as €12.50 for 4 people) because their drivers are totally uninformed about any hotel address and they may get lost/the trip may take 2-3 times more than normal because of their lack of knowledge with hotel addresses.

Coming by train

There are no mainline trains in central Istanbul. Trains to Europe via Bucharest or Sofia historically ran from

Sirkeci station, but this line is disrupted by the Marmaray project and by other work in Bulgaria. There are replacement buses from Sirkeci, at the usual departure time of 10 pm, to link with the westbound train, and returning from the incoming train around 8 am (often very late). As the engineering work grinds on this link has variously been at Halkali at the city's edge, at Cerkezkoy 115 km away, or at Kapikule on the Bulgarian border. The project has been interminably delayed and (as at 2016) no completion is in sight. Sirkeci was also the terminus for international trains to Thessaloniki and regional trains to Edirne and these too are suspended indefinitely (though a daily train runs between Halkali and Edirne). So the station has no trains, but the ticket office remains open. Also just outside is the escalator down to Sirkeci Marmaray station, for the metro across the Bosporus.

You probably need a visa in advance to enter Turkey by train see the note on visas in the section on Ataturk airport.

Trains east to Ankara and beyond historically ran from Haydarpasa, Asian side of the Bosporus, but this closed in 2012. High speed trains ("YHT") now run from Pendik, 25 km east of city centre. The simplest way there is by Marmaray line under the Bosporus then metro to Kartal, then bus 251 or taxi the final 5 km to Pendik station. Allow at least 90 minutes for all this, and note that the first metro of the morning will not get you to Pendik in time for the first Ankara train at 6.30 am. However once Pendik is reached, it has a frequent service to Eskişehir (2 hours) and Ankara (3½ hours), and a twice daily service to Konya (4½ hours). Also Pendik is convenient for Istanbul Sabiha Gokcen airport (10 km, taxi or bus) so consider this route if you intend to fly in and immediately head east. Road transport for Pendik sets down, and picks up to return towards city centre, on the north side of the station. Walk through the subway to south side and turn right for the ticket office, platform access and other station facilities.

For timings and reservations (strongly recommended) see Turkish railways site at tcdd.gov.tr. For destinations in eastern Turkey, take the YHT to Ankara and change, but see that page for disruptions to those services, expected to last till 2018. For Adana, travel via Konya. The international trains to Iran, Syria and Iraq are suspended indefinitely, but the train to Georgia may resume in 2017.

It is not known when the YHT line might be completed from Pendik into the centre of Istanbul, nor whether there will be a single central terminus or separate European and Asian stations as before. But the Marmaray line was designed to take mainline passenger and freight trains as well as the metro.

Coming by bus

Most buses and coaches terminate at the colossal Esenler *Otogar*, about 10 km west of the city center, located on the European side. The station can be easily reached via the Otogar stop on the M1. Companies may also have courtesy minibuses or taxis which will allow you to easily access the center of the city.

Buses depart/arrive for all regions of Turkey as well as for international destinations including cities in Bulgaria, Greece, Republic of Macedonia and Romania. The terminal is huge and each company has a separate office. The area can be a tourist trap with people wanting to help get you to the right office -- for a fee. It is easiest if you know who you want to travel with when you arrive.

With 168 ticket offices and gates, shops, restaurants, hotel, police station, clinic and mosque, the Büyük Otogar is a town in itself. From/To Thessaloniki (Greece): ticket prices are around €45 (one way),€80 with return . From/To Sofia and Varna (Bulgaria): ~30€ (one way). From/To Skopje (Macedonia): ~40€ (one way). Ticket prices may change related with petrol costs but on an avarage 100 kilometers costs 5€ (Euros). Some bus companies selling online tickets from their individual webpages. Varan, Ulusoy,

Pamukkale and KamilKoç are considered as best bus companies of Turkey.

"Harem" is the major hub for the buses on the Anatolian (Asian) side, which can be reached easily from the European side with a Ferryboat.

Turkish bus companies mostly don't have a toilet inside the bus. Buses stop for rest and needs usually every 4 or 5 hours. Rest duration is 30 minutes.

Coming by Boat

International ferries, carrying tourist groups from outside Turkey stop at Karaköy Port. The port is ideally located close to Sultanahmet and Taksim.

Cruise ships often dock close to downtown. Passengers not on tours will find taxis readily available at the port entrance, and modern streetcars a short walk away.

Coming by Var

Traffic in Istanbul can be manic; expect a stressful drive because you will be cut off and honked at constantly.

The city currently holds more than 1,500,000 automobiles and there is a strong demand for building of new or alternate highways.

If you've arrived in Istanbul by car, and you're not familiar with the streets, it's better to park your car in a safe place and take public transportation to get around.

The city, lying on two different continents and separated by the Bosphorus, is connected by two bridges. The bridge on the south, closer to the Marmara Sea, is called the "Bosphorus Bridge". The bridge closer to the Black Sea is named "Fatih Sultan Mehmet Bridge" and is longer than the first one. Both are toll bridges, and you must pay a fee to cross.

Since 2006, the Bosphorus Bridge toll stations do not accept cash, and payment must be made using electronic cards, either manually (KGS) or automatically via a transponder mounted on the front of the car (OGS). The Fatih Sultan Mehmet Bridge does not accept cash either, only KGS or OGS. The minimum amount of credit which can be purchased for a KGS card is 50 Turkish Lyra (October 2012).

On weekdays, drivers should be aware of potentially hour-long traffic jams on the highways leading to both bridges, particularly heading west in the mornings and east in the evenings, since most people live on the Anatolian side but work on the European side.

There is a great shortage of parking in Istanbul, and existing lots are quite expensive. You will see many cars parked on the sides of the road, in front of garage doors even.

Drivers unfamiliar with the city should also be aware that street signs are rare. It is a common thing to pull over and ask for directions, something the natives and taxi drivers do quite often

QuicK Activities Guide

Free Activities

Visit Sinan Pasha Complex, a 4 century-old Ottoman madrasah which is now used as a tourist information center between Beyazit and Cemberlitas tram stations. Tourist-friendly staff provides you with free information about the complex and Turkish-Islamic culture while you are enjoying free refreshments. Don't worry! They don't try to sell you anything! For more information, contact their site.

www.sinanpasha.org

Hamams

See Hamams of Istanbul page for more information on Turkish Bath's in İstanbul. A visit to a *hamam* (Turkish bath) is an essential part of any trip to Istanbul and is something you'll be sure to repeat before leaving. There is at least one historical *hamam* in each neighborhood of Istanbul. Take care in selecting a hamam, as they can vary greatly in cleanliness.

Most places will offer a scrubbing and/or a massage. Just being in the *Hamam* (as a sauna), is enough for seeing and experiencing the place, but the scrubbing is a great experience. The massage is not necessarily better than those found in western countries.

Sultanahmet has many historical hamams. Some are very extravagant and cater mainly to tourists.

An example of a *hamam* frequented by locals is the Buyuk Hamam where a full session (massage plus scrub) will cost you TRY35 instead of the €60 of the tourist ones. The experience is true Turkish so don't expect any western standards.

Aziziye Hamam is on the Asian side of Istanbul. It's a very traditional, clean and cheap Hamam.

Nargile (Hooka/Water Pipe)
Once upon a time, the nargile, or Turkish water pipe, was the centre of Istanbul's social and political life. Today some of the locals still consider it one of life's great pleasures and is something interesting to try. Most of the places where you can smoke a nargile are in Yeniçeriler Caddesi, near the Kapalı Çarşı (Grand Bazaar).

Çorlulu Ali Paşa and Koca Sinan Paşa Türbesi are both in secluded internal courts, just around the corner from some tomb yards, while Rumeli Kahvesi is actually inside the cemetery of an old medrese, though it's not as spooky as you might think. In the south of Sultanahmet, near the sea, is Yeni Marmara (Çayıroğlu Sokak), where you can also sit in the terrace and enjoy the view. In Beyoğlu, at the Ortakahve (Büyükparmakkapı), there's even the choice of a wide range of flavors.

Another area with few big good looking places is the Rıhtım Caddesi, between Galata bridge and Istanbul Modern Museum.

Walking tours
Museums and such: Haghia Sophia, then on to the Topkapı museum (these two should take at least three to five hours), preferably along the road in the back of the Haghia Sophia, where there are some nicely restored houses. Then on to the Blue Mosque and the square with the obelisks on it (At Meydani). Along its

side is the very good Museum of Islam Art. Descend slightly and find the small Haghia Sophia with its nice garden (it was under restoration, but you probably can get in). Then uphill to the Sokollu Mehmet mosque complex, top notch tiles inside.

Take a tram or walk to Eminönü (where the boats leave for trips to Asia or up the Bosphorus). Visit the New Mosque at the back, then the Egyptian Bazaar next to it, and going further in that direction, locate the Rüstem Pasha mosque with its excellent tiles. It's on a raised platform near an old clothes market, you may have to ask directions. Then take a cab or find a bus to Eyüp mosque complex, a mile or three up the Golden Horn. Visit this Eyüp complex at your leisure (the mosque is not particular, the court is, and the milling of believers, with many boys-to-be-circumcised amongst it; a Friday might be a good day to do this).

Then, if you have the stamina, it might be nice to walk back too; maybe all the way (five miles or so), but taking a route along part of the city wall to first the famous Kariye Church with its mosaics, then on to Selimiye Mosque with its great view on the Golden Horn (and a fine mosque by itself), then the Fatih Mosque (passing through some very religious and lively neighbourhoods), then on to the well-restored Sehzade mosque, and next to Süleymaniye (don't forget to enjoy the view from the Golden Horn side). If you have some energy left, you might go on to the University complex, and by then you are very close to the Beyazit mosque. A book market (it's small) is behind this good, unexceptional (nice courtyard though) mosque.

Once again go to Eminönü, but this time take the boat (those large ferries) to Üsküdar. You will arrive before a fine mosque in front, another one four hundred meters off to the right, slightly inland behind a traffic roundabout, and a third, very small, at the sea front. See the market stretching inland, walk about and don't forget to walk along the shore, maybe eating a fish meal in one of the bobbing boats along it. This is a good visit for late afternoon, early evening, fleeing the city. You will be joined by thousands of people going home from "town" but the way back will be on a near-empty ferry. The frequency of ferries will go down in the evening, so make sure there is a connection back.

Go to the railway station and find a Sirkeci-Halkali suburban train, and get out at (from memory, Yedikule station). You will be quite close to Yedikule, a nice fortress, and will have fine views of the city walls. The trains leave every 15 minutes or so, the ride is peculiar (the material is bad, but if you are in luck every second stop another salesman will enter and try selling his wares, it's fun). The ride is takes anywhere from twenty minutes to half an hour. This is not a "must", but it can be great fun.

You will have missed the covered bazaar in all this. That is because you will get there anyhow. If you go to Beyazit and the book market you are almost at two of its many entrances. Try and find the Nuruosmaniye Mosque and its complex at the other side, it's worth it. And after having explored the covered part, take a relaxing walk downhill, into the general direction of Eminönü, where it is "uncovered bazaar" all the way. Cross the Galata bridge to see some things on the Northern side (for instance take the "tünel" teleferik ride up much of the hill (entrance close to the opposite side of Galata bridge, ask around)), then continue to Taksim. Shops are of the international variety.

Theodosian walls walk
From 408 AD the original walls of Constantine were replaced in the reign of Theodosius. These walls then became the critical point of defence of the capital of the Eastern Roman Empire and their Ottoman successors. They are still almost completely intact, marking the western border of the peninsula of Old City, with some sections suffering from somewhat unsightly restoration done in early 1990s. The section around the Topkapı Gate (not to be confused with Topkapı Palace which is located in an altogether different place) can be easily accessed from Pazartekke tram station, which lies about 300 metres east of the

walls. Some remoter sections may not be very safe and may require some caution.

A 7km walk along and on these remaining portions of the city wall offers a window into antiquity and puts emphasis on Turkey's terrible historic monument legacy. Download and print a scholarly historical and technical description of the walls before you visit Istanbul; this will certainly add to the pleasure. From Eminönü, take the Golden Horn ferry to Ayvansaray. This ferry terminal is separate from the Bosphorus terminals adjacent and east of the Galata Bridge. Walk west through the Galata bridge underpass, then through the bus station to a pedestrian laneway which leads to the small terminal building.

The fare is TRY1.50. Leave the ferry at Ayvansaray and cross the park to the wall on the other side of the main road. You have a choice of walking up the outer wall or the inner wall but access to the top of the battlements is usually on the inside naturally enough, so go up the small street across the road which then cuts back behind the wall and the towers. Here you can climb up onto this section of un-restored wall on crumbling brick and stone and continue on some hundreds of yards climbing as necessary. This path comes to an obvious end and one can short cut back to the street. Sometimes there are dwellings and commercial enterprises hard up against the wall, sometimes a bus depot, a rubbish dump or often just the road. These walls replaced the earlier walls of Constantine in 408 AD after which they went through constant upgrade and repairs to earthquake damage.

The different work done over the centuries was all of varying style and quality. Quite surprisingly there are a number of small streets still using the narrow gates. At Hoca Çakır Cd one comes across a restored section of the wall where the heights are accessed by stairs, some along the top of the wall of the steeper variety. This restoration from the 80s is in conflict with the original. The wall is then breached for the main road Fevzi Paşa

Cd. Cross this and continue along the street at the back of the wall.

Look for foot pads and breaks in the wall which allows access and a good look around. The wall is breached again for Adnan Menderes Blv (unofficially and widely known as *Vatan Caddesi*). Past here one see here quite clearly the double line of defence with outer moat. The next breach is for Turgut Özal Cd (unofficially and widely known as *Millet Caddesi*) which hosts the tram line heading back to Sultanahmet for those who have run out of steam. Walking now on the outside of the walls, various breaks in the outer wall allow access via broken stonework or later via modern sets of steps in disrepair. Between the walls is the disquieting evidence of the number of people sleeping rough in Istanbul.

Persevere in staying between the walls because soon you will arrive at another impure restoration project at Mevlanakapı Cd gate. Note that entry to the gate towers has been closed at the gate, so entry is only from the walls. From here it is better to proceed on the outside of the walls because market gardens occupy the moat and the city side abuts buildings. These couple of kms will give a further perspective of the ravages of time and earthquake on the walls. Finally you will arrive at the Golden Gate and Yedikule Fortress which fronts the Marmara Sea and was Byzantium's triumphal point of entry. This is in excellent condition not least because the Ottomans upgraded it and then used it right up to the 19th century. There is an entry fee and it boasts a loo.

The high walls and towers are all accessible, and one tower still has internal wooden floors. So you have now surveyed the protective land walls which kept Byzantium and the Eastern Roman Empire safe for all those years after the fall of Rome, breached only by the 4th Crusaders and the Ottomans. What of their future? Given that recent restoration work is fairly suspect scholars may think it is better to leave them be. Now return to the city either in the Eminönü Bus (#80) from the village square outside the main gate, just wait there, or walk down Yedikule Istasyonu Cd about 300m to the railway line to Sirkeci, both heading for centres close to Sultanahmet.

Bosporus cruise

Around the city you will see various touts for private companies offering Bosporus cruises for €30 or more, often disappointingly short in duration and on rickety boats. A safer, cheaper and more reliable option is to take the official Bosporus cruise from the state-run company Sehir Hatlari which offers a three hour cruise for TRY25 (90 minutes each way with a break of several hours at Anadoli Kavagi) or a shorter non-stop 2 hour cruise for TRY10.

From the Eminönü terminal immediately east of the Galata Bridge starts the large ferry cruising to Anadolu Kavagi at the northern entrance of Bosporus to the Black Sea via various stops. The fare is TRY25. The departure time is early (there are three daily departures during the high season) and is very popular, so arrive early and queue. The open decks are hugely popular, so unless you have an outside seat expect people to be standing all around you constricting the view. The ferry waits some hours in Anadolu Kavagi so as you alight you are confronted by a numerous restaurants and their spruikers.

Firstly take the (very steep) walk to the Yoros Kalesi, a strategic castle overlooking and controlling the entry to the Black Sea. This important fortification with a commanding view has been fought over for many years and was last in use in the 19th century. It has fallen into serious disrepair, but Christian engravings are still visible in the stonework. There are restaurants actually in the castle surrounds and naturally have spectacular views. There is plenty of time left to wander back to the village for lunch. It is late afternoon before arrival back at Eminonu, but a day well spent. A cheaper and faster Bosphorus cruise alternative is a TRY10 trip on a shorter cruise.

Football

Football (soccer) is the most popular sport in Turkey, and Turkish football fans are known for their passion. Many teams from other parts of Europe consider the atmosphere to be very intimidating when they have to play away matches in Turkey. The most intense rivalries in Turkish football are between Beşiktaş , Fenerbahçe , and Galatasaray , and matches between these sides are always played in front of sell-out crowds; getting tickets requires booking way in advance. As the atmosphere is extremely hostile to the away teams, spectators should avoid wearing away team colours after the match, and avoid any signs of crowd trouble.

Learn

Many foreigners visiting or living in Istanbul decide to study Turkish formally in a language school. Some of the biggest and most respected Turkish language schools in Istanbul are:

- ➢ Easy to Transport in Kadıköy.

- ITI Istanbul in 4. Levent.
- A.B.D in 4. Levent.
- EFINST Turkish Center in 1. Levent.
- Dilmer in Gümüşsuyu.
- Tömer, Ankara University affiliated.
- Concept Languages in Etiler.

Boğaziçi University. Runs a summer long intensive Turkish language course for all levels. Both Boğaziçi University and Bilgi University have well established Study Abroad programs in English for foreigners.

Ottoman Turkish

If you already speak Turkish, Ottoman Turkish may also be interesting to learn. Ottoman Turkish was the courtly form of Turkish spoken during the era of the Ottoman Empire, and is significantly different to the form of Turkish spoken today. Approximately 80% of Ottoman Turkish words were loanwords from other languages, mostly Arabic, Persian and French. After the fall of the Ottoman Empire and the establishment of the Republic of Turkey, language reforms were implemented, including the establishment of the *Türk Dil Kurumu* (Turkish Language Association), which is the official regulatory body of the Turkish language. This association, with a philosophy of linguistic purism, decided to cleanse the Turkish language of loanwords and replace them with more Turkic alternatives. As such, only about 14% of modern Turkish words are of foreign origin.

Ottoman Turkish is the key to learning about Turkey's Ottoman past. With Ottoman Turkish, not only can you read historical archives, but you can also read Ottoman literature and letters dated back to the Ottoman period.

Working

There is always demand for qualified ESOL/EFL teachers in Istanbul. Most teachers work with private instructional companies or private schools. Private schools are notorious for the spoiled, nouveau riche families that send their children there and remember:

you, the teacher, are always wrong and the student always right at such establishments. The days when a would-be English teacher teacher without a certificate could get a job, however, are long gone, even for under the table jobs. While Istanbul may seem charming to a first-time visitor, actually living in a city that has far more people than it was designed to support is simply excruciating after a while, and the turnover rate is exceptionally high. Also keep in mind that the market is quite saturated. You will probably find a job, but not a very good one at first. Making contacts is key. Some English teachers work under the table and pay is generally enough to live on. Some university English preparatory schools at institutions such as Sehir, Koc, Sabanci and a few other private schools, provide decent salaries, and about 10 to 50 percent -- if you are frugal -- can be saved. State universities have higher quality, more motivated students, but pay as little as half their private counterparts, albeit with more holiday time.

Late payment is not uncommon, and there are plenty of horror stories of bosses cheating their employees.

If you want to live and teach in Turkey, a calmer alternative is to live in a smaller city where you will be in higher demand and the cost of living is lower. However, cultural and entertainment opportunities can be limited, especially for women.

Buying

Connecting east and west, the will to control the major trading routes was the reason why Istanbul was founded in the first place, so shopping should definitely not be overlooked in your Istanbul experience.

The currency used in Istanbul is the Turkish Lira (TL or TRY) though the euro and US dollar are also accepted at places frequented by tourists (although certain tourist attractions such as the Hagia Sophia only accept liras). Currency exchanges (*döviz bürosu*) and banks are plentiful in Istanbul and offer extremely competitive exchange rates with no commission charged. If you are planning to visit Istanbul, bring hard foreign currency and exchange them after you arrive, preferably at a bank or a currency exchange. Exchange only what you need as you will find difficulty exchanging your leftover TL back to foreign currency after you leave the country. Alternatively, withdraw money from ATMs whenever you need cash.

Shops may be closed on Sundays. Most major shopping malls have security checkpoints you usually see in airports and museums prior to entry.

Istanbul's historical bazaars with an oriental ambience, once sitting firmly on the western terminii of the Silk Road and spice routes, all dating back to Ottoman era, are all located in the the peninsula of Old City. However, expect extreme price rises in the Grand Bazaar as it's become a mere tourist attraction. Just moving by few meters outside of it you can see prices drop quickly. If you plan on shopping a lot, a flight to Gaziantep (which can be quite cheap) may be worth it.

On the other hand, modern shopping malls (*alışveriş merkezi*, usually shortened to *AVM*), popping all around the city in the last three decades, are mostly to be found in New Istanbul and western suburbs, though they are by no means exclusively located in these districts.

If you are after top quality upmarket garments, then you may better head for Nişantaşı in European Side and Bağdat Avenue in Asian Side.

Here are some of what are popular to buy while in the city:

Turkish Delight, or Lokum (as the locals call it). A good buy since you're in Turkey. It is advisable to buy it fresh rather than in pre-packed boxes and to get a variety of flavours rather than the stereotypical rose-water or lemon flavors available abroad. Pistachio in particular is very good. The best place to buy lokum in Istanbul is from a store. Istiklal Caddesi in particular features a number of stores that sell Turkish sweets by the kilogram including lokum and helvah. There are quite a few shops selling Turkish Delight in the Grand Bazaar, although unless you are very good at haggling better prices can be found elsewhere. Highly recommended for Lokum is the Malatya Pazari stall in the Spice Market. The Turkish delight there was fresh, had great flavors including some offbeat ones and the prices were fair.

DO NOT BUY the 10 TL Turkish delight boxes (the ones that come sealed sold in any tourist shop or all along Istiklal Avenue). Once you get home and open them, it is a major disappointment. It is much less quantity than the what look like as the size of the box and it tastes horrible. Only buy the ones that you can taste before hand and you see what they are putting inside the box. It will be probably twice the price, but it shall be worthwhile.

There are two kinds of lokums. The first kind is the ones that are made with sugar and sold in small pieces. As of April 2016, these are about 40 TRY per kg. The second kind is the ones that are made with honey. They usually look like a long stick then cut in to pieces when you buy them. The prices are vary depending on where you buy them. Some people mention that spice market is the best place to buy, but it is also most expensive place to buy, about 95 TRY per kg. Even the oldest lokum shop in Istanbul, Ali Muhiddin Haci Bekir (founded 1777 in Ottoman period), sells for 85 TRY per kg. But no one really goes there any more. Hafiz Mustafa is one of the most popular lokum shops that both locals and tourists go. It has many locations. The price, as of April 2016, is around 85 TRY per kg. I recommend Baklavaci Muhammed Said. It is not as old as others but it is a family run business, has the best quality, and yet still keeps the cheapest price too. (As of April 2016, 65 TRY per kg)

Turkish Tea (çay, CHAI). The national drink of Turkey, brewed from leaves grown on the steep, verdant mountain slopes of Turkey's eastern Black Sea coast. Traditionally, Turkish tea is brewed samovar-style, with a small pot of very strong tea sitting on a larger vessel of boiling water. Pour a small amount of strong tea into a little tulip-shaped glass and cut it to the desired strength with hot water. Turks usually add cube sugar (never milk, although you can often get milk if you ask.) Having fresh, hot tea always available everywhere is one of life's splendid little luxuries in Turkey. Elma Çay: apple tea, like hot apple juice (EHL-mah chah-yee) is the flavour of preference, although it's more for tourists; Turks prefer Siyah Çay (black tea).

Rugs and kilims can be a good buy while in the city. Most rug-specialized stores in the city, though, are aimed at tourist trade, so pick up basics of haggling to avoid being ripped off at these stores. They are mostly located around Sultanahmet.

Chalcedony. A semi-precious gemstone named after the near-by town of Chalcedon, and is sold in many of Istanbul's multitude of jewellery shops.

Off the Beaten Path. Places that offer the best at what they do but are not on any of the traditional tourist paths.

ArkeoPera, Yenicarsi Caddesi, 16/A Petek Han, Galatasaray, +90 212 2930378 . Best antiquarian bookshop in Turkey, owner knows every Turkish excavation site first hand.

Gonul Paksoy, 6/A Atiye Sokak, Tesvikiye, +90 212 2360209. Peerless one-of-a-kind dresses made for royalty from refined, antique Ottoman-era cloth.

Iznik Foundation, 7 Oksuz Cocuk Sokak, Kurucesme, +90 212 2873243. Offers neo-Iznik pottery after recreating original formulas from original Iznik kilns, which functioned between 1450 and 1650.

Sedef Mum, 50 Irmak Caddesi, Dolapdere, +90 212 2535793. Artisans of the time honoured art of candle making, intricately sculpted and aromatic wares make very portable gifts.

Real Estate. Places in Fatih since 1990 to buy or rent every type real estate.

Yiğitsan, Üniversite Mh. Bağlariçi Cad. No: 35

Kuruoğlu gayrimenkul, Akşemsettin Mahallesi, Fevzipaşa Caddesi, No:11, Dinçay Han, Fatih, +90 212 5240108 . Old real Estate office in Fatih in İstanbul since 1990 with two branches.

Teksen Çamlıbel, Ota Jinemed Nüzhetiye Cad. Deryadil Sk. No:1 Beşiktaş / İstanbul, +90 444 3 802 .

Eating

For individual restaurant listings, check district articles.

When having a look for a restaurant, there will be a lot of restaurants, where the staff will try to make one come inside. There is really a kind of competition between the restaurants to make one come inside. However, the best restaurants are not always the expensive tourist restaurants, but those small Lokantas where even the turkish people go for having dinner.

Snacks

Döner. Always a good option for having fast and cheap food. The entrance to Istiklal Street contains dozens of small doner restaurants and they serve almost around the clock; though for a better experience (and a better food quality) you may want to wander about in residential neighbourhoods, since anything near a commercial or tourist area can be highly overpriced and greatly reduced in quality.

Balık-Ekmek. Balik-Ekmek (literally "fish and bread") is a fish sandwich served in small boats and little buffets in Eminonu. It is also increasingly popular in buffets in Kadıköy coast. A regular sandwich consists of one small fried fish, slices of tomatoes and onion. However, the taste is beyond expectations for such a basic menu. The price 6 TL right off the docks at Eminou. Again, it's a local favorite.

Hamsi. In Autumn and Winter the Black Sea Anchovy migrate through the Bosphorus, the local fishermen coming out in force to take advantage. All fish restaurants have them on the menu in season. It seems the classic serving is a handful of deep fried fish with raw onion and bread. Eat the fish whole, it's a winner. Look for the small restaurants behind the fish merchants on the Karakoy side of the Galata Bridge, western side. Expect to pay TL8.

Patso. Patso is a type of sandwich consisting of hot dog and french fries. It's usually served in small buffets along the Uskudar coast and a sandwich costs 1.50 TL. The cheap price can raise eyebrows but these buffets are open 24/7 and they serve around 1000 sandwiches per day. Even though the profit margin is low, they make a fortune, so they don't lower the quality too much (except hamburgers, don't touch those in Uskudar, but definitely try the spicy hamburgers in Taksim).

One thing not to be missed is the local ice cream sold at the street stands, called dondurma. While flavors are relatively standard for the region, the ice cream usually incorporates orchid root extract, which gives it an incredibly chewy and stringy texture, also lending itself to be used for marketing and attracting attention while the sellers do tricks to try to sell the ice cream. Try it!

Kumpir is a snack which can easily be a full meal. It is originated from Albania but is quite unique to Istanbul in its present form. It consists of a baked potato with various fillings such as grated cheese, mayonnaise, ketchup, pickles, sweetcorn, sausage slices, carrots, mushrooms, and Russian salad among others, any of which can optionally be added to or omitted from the mix. While kumpir can be had at many cafes throughout the city, it is best had from one of the cafes in Ortaköy, which have a long tradition of preparing kumpir and offer really filling and tasty ones. About 8 TL each.

Roasted chestnuts("kestane Kebap, as locals call it) are sold from carts around the city, and is a very nice snack to have when the weather is cold, as it keeps your hands warm. Quality and flavour is generally good but can vary Between batches, even from the same stand. 5Lr for 100 grams, 10Lr for 200 grams and so on - same prices citywide.

Boiled and roasted corn on the cob (known as Süt Misir and Közde Misir in Turkish, respectively) is sold from carts around the city, and is a fantastic snack to walk around. Price varies from cart to cart and area of the city. 2 Lr.

Don't miss the "simit," a warm bread sold from carts around the city, and is a fantastic snack to walk around. The texture and taste is a bit like a sesame bagel. 1 Lr.

Also, be sure to try Ayran, a local drink based on yoghurt, although sour and much thinner. It isn't always on the menu or displayed, but it's there, so ask for it. 2Lr.

Freshly squeezed juice and juice blends are sold from stands and small shops all around the city, and are a refreshing treat (especially in the warmer months). The combinations range from a simple orange juice to the more rare options like pomengranate or kiwi. Price varies from shop to shop, area of the city and complexity of your order (between 2 and 4 Lr).

Drink

Beyoğlu is notoriously known for its night life; it's full of cafes and bars with live music. People from all classes and ethnicities can be found here.

Nişantaşı is the place for young entrepreneurs and artists, the prices are higher than Taksim.

Kadıköy also has a nightlife scene, serving mostly locals of this part of the city. It is usually has more easy-going style of nightlife, usually with local pubs and wine houses and traditional meyhanes. If you are not staying on that side of the city, it may not worth the trouble to make an inter-continental trip just to have a drink, but drop by if you are around and thirsty.

Nightclubs - While there are night clubs all over the city, two of the hottest clubs of Istanbul are in Ortaköy.

Istanbul/Galata A local hotspot for those who want to avoid the clubs of Taksim. The steps going down from the Galata Tower are heaving at night so grab some beers/raki from the local shops and an interesting mix of about 90% local to 10% tourist.

Sleep

In general, it's possible to find some kind of accommodation in any district of Istanbul. Here's a quick list of the districts where there are the greatest concentrations of lodgings:

Harbiye is a popular place to stay, as in the main centre of the new city on the European side, and contains a variety of international standard apartments, hotels, and moderate hotels for budget travellers. Nişantaşı and Taksim are 5 minutes from Harbiye so you can stay in Harbiye and benefit from all activities in Nişantaşı and Taksim.

Taksim is the main centre of the new city on the European side. Locals and tourists go to Taksim for shopping and entertainment, as well as moderate hotels for budget travellers. There are also two hostels in this area.

Sultanahmet the main centre for the old city on the European side. It has a selection of quality, reasonably priced hotels, many with terraces overlooking the Golden Horn, or with views of the Marmara Sea and the Blue Mosque. Most hostel-type accommodation frequented by independent travellers are located in this district, although it is possible to find a few upmarket hotels.

Quite pricey hotels can be found in western suburbs, especially around the airport, as well as on/overlooking the banks of Bosphorus.

With the closure of relatively central Ataköy caravan park, the place where you can tow your caravan nearest to the city is now located in Selimpaşa, a far outer western suburb of the city, though it is still a good 40km away from central parts of the city.

Avrasya Hostel, Cankurtaran Mahallesi Seyit Hasan Sokak No:12, Sultanahmet, Istanbul, Turkey, +902125169380. Avrasya Hostel is a family owned hostel in the centre of Sultanahmet. Its central location makes it an ideal place to stay in the city and explore all the prime attractions by foot. They have a nice open terrace where they serve breakfast. from USD 8.

Contact

Emergency numbers
Dial 155 for police, 110 for fire, 112 or 911 for medical

Telephone codes
Istanbul is the only city/province in Turkey which has more than one telephone code: 212 for European side, 216 for Asian side and Princes' Islands. When calling from one continent to the other, the usual dialing format used for intercity calls should be used, as if it's an intercity call: *0+area code (212 or 216)+7-digit telephone number*. It may appear as an intercity call, but it will be treated as a local call in respect to payment. When making an intercontinental call, if you

forget to dial the code, your call will *not* be automatically routed to the other continent number, it is likely that you will be connected to the "wrong" number which is in the same continent with you, because much of the number sets are used on both continents (albeit with different codes of course). When dialing a number that is on the continent you are already standing on, only 7-digit number is enough. Don't forget to dial the code first no matter which continent you are in if you are calling a landline number from a cell phone (even if it's a number that is in the same continent with you), though.

SIM Cards

Prepaid SIM cards can be bought (for around 30 TL with 5TL usable balance) at Vodafone, Avea or Turkcell kiosks at the airport or in shops around town. At the Airport, the Avea, Vodafone and Turkcell shops are respectively to the left, right and across from the exit. For about 90TLY Avea offers a 250 minute in Turkey, 100 minute to Europe, 1GB of data plan, the other two have similar plans. Ask the salesperson to set it up for you and check by calling his phone and opening up a webpage. For iPhone, it may be necessary to download Turkish script before the phone can be used. They ask to make a copy of your passport.

However, to be able to use your phone you need to get it unlocked for use in Turkey. With a bit of luck the guy in the shop can do it for you, though that may violate the rules of your contract, depending on the country you are from. Having your phone unlocked officially can happen through your operator in your home country.

Internet

Cafés with free wireless internet (wi-fi):

- ➢ Several of the nargile places in Tophane
- ➢ Several cafes in Cihangir, including Kahvedan, Meyva, Komşufırın and Kahve Altı
- ➢ Many cafés and restaurants along Istiklal Caddesi in Beyoglu

- Both the large American fast food restaurant chains
- There is one upstairs by the restaurants facing the side of Aya Sofia and behind the entrance to the Basilica in Sultanahmet.
- Starbucks has quite a few shops around, and (at least) those at the touristic zones, has a free wireless connection.

In the recent years, the number of cafes and shopping centers with wi fi Internet access has increased dramatically, most of them still being free. Most internet cafes have high speed ADSL connections, and they are very inexpensive compared to Europe (about 0.50-1.50 Euros per hour).

- Most hostels and hotels of the Sultanahmet area have wi-fi Internet access in thier lobby, and often in the rooms. They can be overpriced, though.

Wi-Fi

Hotel Every hotel has their own Wi-Fi. Some hotels do have trouble with their network setup or the connection due to the historical location however at the least you will have free wi-fi at your hotel. All you have to do is to learn the wifi password to access the internet.

Cafes Every café, bistro, restaurant share their internet with their guests. Even the small restaurants now have internet access. Stability and speed depend on where you are and what kind of café, bistro or restaurant you are in. Starbucks, Nero etc. typically have stable wi-fi unless very crowded. If you are in a Starbucks all you have to do is connect your device (SSID should be TTNET or DorukNet, AND if you are in Nero DorukNet) and fill out some basic information for verification that you have to fill. After that, you are ready to go. And if you are in the other restaurant or cafés you can just ask to your waiter to get SSID and Password and after that you are ready to go.

Public Center and Squares Municipality of Istanbul recently announced that free public wi-fi will be available in most common city centers and squares. All you have to do is (when you near of one of these centers of course) register your id via your cell phone and you will get an access password.

Wi-Fi on the Go You can rent a mobile wifi hotspot during your stay in Turkey. It works based on 3G connection in the whole country, and you can connect up to 10 devices at the same time. These pocket-sized devices can be easily booked online.

While there are plenty of international companies that rent a mobile hotspot, mainly three local companies are operating:

- Alldaywifi
- Rent 'n Connect

Stafety

As with most European cities, but especially in crowded areas of Istanbul, watch your pockets and travel documents as pickpockets have devised all sorts of strategies to obtain them from you. Do not rely too much on the 'safe' feeling you get from the omnipresence of policemen. Taksim Square, Sultanahmet Square, Istiklal Avenue, Kadikoy Square etc. are observed by security cameras monitored by police 24/7 non-stop.

Also be wary of men in Taksim who splash water on the backs of your neck. When you turn around, they will try to start a fight with you as another man comes in and robs you. These men tend to carry knives and can be very dangerous.

Slums which host number of scammers are located between Suleymaniye and Ataturk avenue. Appearance in these areas even during daylight could result in aggressive behavior of locals who could try to throw away strangers from their territory. Avoiding these dangerous urban blocks is highly recommended.

Istanbul is home to three of the biggest clubs in Turkey and arguably European football: Beşiktaş, Fenerbahçe, and Galatasaray. It is advisable not to wear colours associating yourself with any of the clubs--black and white, blue and yellow, and red and yellow, respectively--particularly on the days of matches between the sides due to the fearsome rivalry they share.

Be respectful of the Turkish flag. Don't put it on places where people sit or stand, don't drag it, don't wrinkle it, don't contaminate it, don't use it as a dress or uniform. Not only will Turks be very offended, furthermore the desecration of the Turkish flag is a punishable offence. The flag is extremely important and well respected in Turkey.

Scams

Below are scams that have been reported. They may be discouraging; however, of all these scams, the most common is the overpriced taxis, which also happens to be the most common scam in the world. In other words, use traveler's common sense and caution and you'll be safe. And do not be afraid of the police; if you think you are being scammed or robbed, the police will take the utmost care of you.

Blue Mosque scam "guides

When walking through the gates of the Blue Mosque, beware of smiling, friendly chaps who offer immediately to be your de-facto guide through the mosque and its surroundings; while they are informative on just about anything relating to the mosque--etiquette, history, Islamic practices--they eventually demand a price for their "services", a quotation that can be as high as 50TL (about EUR 25 or GBP 20). One would be better off booking a private tour online; or not at all, since the mosque is free to all anyway.

For Hagia Sophia it is, however, reasonable, especially if you travel within a group, to use guide's services. Since the audio-guides cost 20 TL p.p. it could be even cheaper with a guide. He will also put you straight to the ticket office so you don't have to wait on a line. Just be careful, when negotiating the price, that he will require 50 TL as a whole, and not per person.

There are also many 'helpful guys' in the area who will let you know that the Blue Mosque is closed, either for prayers or some other reason. While the prayer hall may be closed briefly at such times, the mosque courtyard remains open all day and well into the evening, and you can happily sit there and enjoy the surroundings while you wait for prayers to finish, if indeed they are happening. These guys are really just agents for carpet and art dealers who will happily lead you away from the sights to their shop. Always ignore them. Honest Turkish people will not approach strangers unless they are in evident need of assistance.

Bar/club scams
Be aware of high-drink price scams in "night-clubs" (located mostly in Aksaray, Beyazit and Taksim areas). These clubs can charge overpriced bills (hundreds or thousands of lira) based on a replica of the original

menu or even simply a menu lying upside down on the table.

Be especially aware of "friendly" young men/groups of young men/male-female couples inviting you to a "good nightclub they know"---this is frequently a prelude to a scam. Scammers often work to earn your trust, striking up a conversation or even taking you to a legitimate restaurant and covering the bill. In another variation, the scammer will talk to you in Turkish, and when you reply in your own language, they will be "surprised" you're not Turkish and offer to repay you for their accident with a beer. Note that some scammers are very, very patient, working for hours to gain your trust before finally taking you to a bar.

The conversations may start very naturally that you may lose your scene of awareness. Scammers may dress very smart and look high educated. They also pretend to be a tourist like you, not the local with the same interest to discover Istanbul and inviting you too. Believe me, you will be surprised with various ways of stating a conversation with you: "Do you have a lighter? Could you help me to take a photo?... In the middle of a walking conversation, they may stop in an exchange office to change some Euros to Lira just to make you believe that they are also tourists like you. Normally, the key question to get 'access' to you is "Where are you from?".

In any of these scams, if you refuse to pay the high prices or try to call the police (dial #155), the club managers may resort to physical intimidation. In general, use caution: scams in Taksim are becoming more serious, and organized crime may be involved.

The following tips will not guarantee protection from bar/club scams, but may help you avoid the most common traps:

➤ <u>Beware of unsolicited advice or conversation from "locals."</u> The best option is to ignore such conversation and move to a more populated/well-lit area, *no matter how "friendly" the "local" seems.*

- <u>Be aware of friendly "Tourists" as well</u>. They may be very talent actors/actresses and you only realise this when you receive a very high bill from the bar that you go together with them.

- <u>Beware of bars and clubs where you seem to be the only tourist</u>. In addition, any bar that looks like it could be a strip club is likely a scam joint.

- <u>Always ask for the exact price of drinks before ordering</u>. Of course, scammers will not be honest, but any hesitation, evasiveness, or ambiguity is a good sign of foul play.

- <u>Remember the location of nearby public areas with lots of people (preferably police)</u>. The best place to get away from scammers is in a crowd monitored by law enforcement.

- <u>Carry only minimal cash</u>. If the scammer takes your money, you can cut your losses. Some scammers will even escort you to an ATM to obtain more cash; if the ATM is in a public area, it will be easier to get the attention of law enforcement.

- <u>Never indicate where you are staying</u>. The last thing you need is for the scammers to follow you to your own bed.

If you are caught by scammers and faced with an impossible bill, keep the following in mind:

- The safest option is to comply with the scammers while finding a way to get out of the situation.
- When possible, head to a safe (i.e., public) place and call the police (dial #155).
- There are many police in Taksim and other public areas, including undercover operatives. Do not be shy about yelling "Polis! Polis!" (Police! Police!). The police will be very willing to assist, and younger police are generally

university graduates capable of some English or German.

➢ Suggest that you need to visit an ATM; this will give you a chance to leave the club, head to a more public area, and attract the attention of police.

➢ In a few situations, tourists have run away when faced with an exorbitant bill. This is risky, due to the physical fitness required as well as possible physical retaliation should the attempt fail. However, those who succeed follow the basic strategy listed above: comply with the scammers until you find an opportunity to get away, and head towards a public area with police.

Lira/Euro Scams

A frequent scam, often in smaller hotels (but it can also happen in a variety of other contexts), is to quote prices in Lira and then later, when payment is due, claim the price was given in Euros. Hotels which reject payment early in a stay and prefer you to "pay when you leave" should raise suspicions. Hotels which operate this scam often offer excellent service and accommodation at a reasonable price and know most guests will conclude as much and pay without complaint - thus (ironically) this can be a sign of a good hotel.

Another scam is, as you walk across the streets, a guy with his wife and a cute kid would come and abruptly hit on you giving handshakes and exchanging greetings. They will identify your nationality/region somehow and will talk about your region's famous actors/singers and make you feel comfortable. Then they will talk about your currency and ask how much of your currency is worth one dollar or one lira. They will very politely request you to show them your currency notes. The moment you open your wallet, the guy would very gently put his hands on the wallet pretending to just see all the possible denominations. Meanwhile his wife or himself would talk something else to divert your attention and your largest 2 denominations would disappear. This is purely con-art and is very common in Eminonu square, Taksim square and is reported by Asian looking people.

Another scam is coin-related and happens just as you're walking into the streets. A Turkish guy holds you and asks where you are from. If you mention a Euro-country, the guy wants you to change a €50 note from you into two-Euro coins he is showing. He is holding the coins stack-wise in his hands. For the trouble, he says he will offer you '30 two-Euro coins, making €60 in total'. Do not agree with this exchange of money, as the first coin is indeed a two-Euro coin, but (many of) the rest of the coins will probably be 1 Lira coins (looking very similar), but worth only 1/4 of the value of €2.

Many bars in the Taksim area give you counterfeit bills. They are usually well-made and hard to identify as fakes in the dark. One way to verify its authenticity is to check its size against another bill. Another is to hold the bill up to a strong light, face side up, and check for an outline of the same face which is on the bill. The value of the bill (20, 50, etc) should appear next to the outline, light and translucent. If either if these two security features are missing, try to have the bill changed or speak to the police.

Fake Currency

Some currency exchanges might give you fake turkish lira notes. Try to see whether the numbers of the notes are different, although if only one out of many is fake, it will be hard to recognise. Usually newer notes should be looked at with a suspicious eye, especially if the silver part of the note is very reflective and colorful.

One currency exchange in Taksim area on the road to the left of Istiklal street (the one with Ottoman palace hotel and Hafiz Mustafa) has placed 2 fake notes in the middle of real ones. It would be wise to avoid him, (First currency exchange on the road leading southwards, left of istiklal street).

Also happens at Metro stations, with a helpful person offering to help with the ticket machines (they are slightly complicated!) and then asks for smaller change for his large "fake" note.

Shoebrush
Some people will walk around Taksim (or other tourist-frequented areas) with a shoeshine kit, and the brush will fall off. This is a scam to cause some Western tourist with a conscience to pick it up and return it to the owner, who will then express gratitude and offer to shine your shoes for free. While doing that, he will talk about how he is from another city and how he has a sick child. At the end, the shiner will demand a much higher price for the "free" services provided than is the actual market norm.

Another type of scam is used especially by children-shoebrushers. On rainy days they act like they dropped and broke their shoeshine kit and literally paint the floor, then they start to cry and sob. Then, they wait for some emotional people (especially tourists) to help them and/or pay them.

If you actively decide that you would like your shoes shined, then expect to pay not more than 5 lira for both.

Taxi drivers
Taxis are plentiful in Istanbul and inexpensive by Western European and American standards. They can be picked up at taxi hubs throughout the city or on the streets. Empty cabs on the streets will honk at pedestrians to see if they would like a ride, or cabs can be hailed by pedestrians by making eye contact with the driver and waving. Few taxi drivers speak languages other than Turkish, but do a fair job at deciphering mispronounced location names given by foreign riders. It is advisable to have the name of the destination written down and try to have a map beforehand to show the driver, to avoid any misunderstanding and also potential scams. Though taxis are plentiful, be aware that taxis are harder to

find during peak traffic hours and traffic jams and when it is raining and snowing. They are also less frequent during nights, depending on the area and and are hard to find after midnight.

Try to avoid using taxis for short distances (5-10 minutes of walk) if possible. Some taxi drivers can be annoyed with this, especially if you called the cab from a taxi hub instead of hailing it from the street. If you want taxis for short distances, just hail them from the street, do not go to the taxi hub.

Few taxis have seatbelts, and some drivers may seem to be reckless. If you wish for the driver to slow down, say "yavash lütfen" (slow please). Your request may or may not be honored.

Unfortunately, as in any major city, tourists are more vulnerable to taxi scams than locals. Be aware that taxi drivers use cars affiliated with a particular hub, and that the name and phone number of the hub, as well as the license plate number, are written on the side of each car. Noting or photographing this information may be useful if you run into problems. In general, riding in taxis affiliated with major hotels (Hilton, Marriot, Ritz, etc.) is safe, and it is not necessary to stay in these hotels to use a taxis leaving from their hubs.

Others may take unnecessarily long routes to increase the amount due (although sometimes alternate routes are also taken to avoid Istanbul traffic, which can be very bad). Some scams involve the payment transaction; for example, if the rider pays 50 TL when only 20 TL are needed, the driver may quickly switch it with a 5 TL note and insist that the rest of the 20 TL is still due or may switch the real bill for a fake one and insist that different money be given.

Methods to avoid taxi scams:

1. SIT IN THE FRONT PASSENGER SEAT. Watch the meter. Watch the driver's actions (beeping the horn, pumping the brakes, etc) and note what the taximeter

does. Try to avoid putting your luggage in the boot. While it is rare, some drivers will wire parts of their controls to increase the fare upon activation. If you're with your significant other, do it anyway. Save the cuddling for after the ride. Check if the seal on the taximeter is broken. Use your phone for light. This will make the driver realize that you are cautious. Be very careful when the driver touches the meter or when you can't see the meter. Challenge the driver right away to see if there's any unusual jumps in the price. Note that for women it is better to sit in the back seat (where you can see the meter from the middle), as there are occassionally problems with taxi drivers getting overly friendly, and sitting in the front is a sign that a woman welcomes such behavior.

2. Ask "How much to go to...?" (basic English is understood), before getting in the taxi. Price will be quite accurate to the one in the taximeter at the end of the ride. If the price sounds ok for you, get in the cab and tell them to put the Taximeter on. Since 2009, the

rate they are applying is same during night and day. Also you can use this useful and up-to-date cab fare estimation tool for Istanbul:

3. Know the route. If you have a chance, find a map and demand that the driver take your chosen route to the destination. Often times they will drive the long way or pretend not to know where you're going in order to get more money out of you. If the driver claims not to know the route to a major landmark or gathering place, refuse his services as he is likely lying.

4. Choose an elderly driver. Elderly taxi drivers are less likely to cheat passengers.

5. Let taxi driver see money on your hands and show values and take commitment on it. This is 50 Lira. OK? Take this 50 Lira and give 30 Lira back OK?. This guarantees your money value. Otherwise, your 50 Lira can be 5 Lira immediately on his hands. Try to have always 10 Lira or 20 Lira bills in your wallet. This makes money scams in general more difficult. If you realize

that the driver tried to use the 50 Lira to 5 Lira trick on you, call the police (#155) immediately and write down the license plate.

6. Create a big scene if there is a problem. If you are absolutely positive you have been subject to a scam, threaten to or call the police and, if you feel it will help, start yelling. Taxi drivers will only rip off those they think will fall for it; creating a scene draws attention to them and will make it easier to pay the correct rate.

7. This taxi just scammed me in Taksim Square Plate number 34 THD 86 >:(add more plate numbers here everyone!!

Overpricing
Watch the menu carefully in street cafes for signs that prices are not discriminatory if prices are clearly overinflated, simply leave. A good indication of over inflation is the circulation of two different types of menu the "foreigner" menu is typically printed on a laminated card with menu prices written in laundry marker/texta, i.e., prices not be printed; in these cases,

expect that prices for foreigners will be highly inflated (300% or higher).

While this is not really a problem in Beyoğlu or Ortaköy, avoiding the open air cafes toward the rear courtyard of the Spice Bazaar (Sultanahmet) is wise. The area immediately north of the Spice Bazaar is also crawling with touts for these 'infamous' cafes.

Having nargile (water pipe) is a famous activity in Istanbul. Tophane (top-hane) is a famous location for this activity where a huge number of nargile shops are available and can easily be reached by the tram, avoiding a place called "Ali Baba" in Tophane is wise, usually you will be served there with plates you did not ask for like a nuts plate, and expect to have a bill of around $50 for your nargile!

You should be carefull also when ordering food in some restaurants. For example, in a restaurant called "Konak Kebap", located in Istiklal street, the waiter will take your order in English and then ask about the size of the portions in a confusing mixture of Turkish, Arabic and/or English. In that way, you will very probably ask for larger portions or non-wanted extras that will raise the price of the bill more than 300%. For example, a "medium" kebap has the same price as 4 normal kebaps (the menu only shows the price of the normal portions). Avoiding "Konak kebap" in Istiklal; and Kebap Saray in Takseem Square is wise. You should also be careful in other restaurants near touristic areas, to avoid any surprises.

Getting around inside Istanbul
Public transport

Istanbul's public transit system can be difficult to figure out; maps are rare and you often have to transfer, and pay another fare, to get where you are going. However, if you put some effort into it, you can avoid taxis and not walk too much.

There is an extensive bus system, including city-run and private buses, as well as one high-speed *Metrobüs* line;

an extensive light rail system including four *Metro* (underground) lines, four *Tramvays* (aboveground), two *Fünikülers* (ascending/descending), two mini-lines called *Teleferik*, and the *Marmaray* (underwater) lines; and the ferries which travel the Bosphorus.

An important supplement to all of this (particularly late at night) is the fleet of private *dolmuş* minivans, which follow prescribed routes and wait until they fill up before departing. They range in price from 2-8 lira (paid in cash), depending on how far you're going. They run all night long, unlike most of the public transport lines. So if you find yourself stranded at Taksim at 4am, a dolmuş is your way home. Look for the yellow minivans, and ask them where they're going ("néreye gidiyórsunuz?").

Each time you use a tram, metro, bus, or boat on the public transport system, you will need to use a token (expensive) or a magnetic card (cheaper, see below). The small metal/plastic tokens cost 4 TL (July 2014) and can be bought at various ticket kiosks & machines at bus, railway and metro stations. Ticket fares across buses, trams and metros are at a flat rate (i.e. not dependent on how far you go). Only cash in Turkish lira is accepted at ticket kiosks of public transport, no credit cards or foreign currency. Also be aware that the Istanbul subway system does not offer transfer tickets and as such each new line requires a new fare, unless you use an an Istanbulkart or Akbil (see below).

Istanbulkart

Buying an Istanbulkart is a good idea if you are in Istanbul for more than a day or two, and intend to use public transport. This is a plastic card that looks like a credit card. It can be used as a ticket on buses, trams, suburban trains, metro, some cross-Bosphorus ferries, and even some public toilets. You touch the Istanbulkart to a reader when you get on the bus or enter the tram/metro platform. The great part for groups of travellers is that you can buy only one and touch it as many times as there are passengers (unlike

London's *Oyster* card, there is no need to *touch out*). You can buy or refill them at designated booths located at any major bus, tram, to metro station, as well as some other places such as newspaper stands close to bus stops.

An Istanbulkart provides a flat fare of 2.60TL for the first ride, which is a cheaper option in comparison to tokens used in Metro and speed trams (jeton, 4TL). It is also 3,85TL to the Prince's Islands, instead of 6TL for a token, 4,15TL to Sabiha Gökçen airport instead of 5TL. Istanbulkart also allows discounts in transfers, 1.80 TL for second trip and 1.40 for third trip etc., within roughly an hour and a half since the last time you used it). Card-issuing machines don't give any change, so anything above the deposit of 6 TL (non-refundable) will be initial balance of the card. Note that there are different booths for buying the card and for charging it, and charging booths accept only 5, 10, and 20 lira banknotes.

Once you have bought and loaded the card, your first journey costs 2.60TL (except for Metrobus, which costs around 3TL). Then, any change within approximately 2 hours costs progressively cheaper: the second journey is 1.80TL, the third is 1.40TL etc. (fares accurate as of Jun 2018). When several people are traveling using one card, the fare paid for the second, third etc. passengers may differ. Note that changing metro line or travel type, i.e., ferry to bus, or metro to tram, requires you to go out of the turnstiles and then back in to the new line or travel type. Therefore, this is extremely more economical than buying individual *jetons* at 4TL per journey.

The Istanbulkard has been in use since 2015 or earlier, having replaced the older *Akbil* metal touch-token. Some Kiosks still have *Akbil* signs rather than *Istanbulkart* signs - but you can usually buy or top up your Istanbulkart at any kiosk where the *Akbil* sign is displayed.

By bus

IETT

There are two types of public buses in Istanbul; those run by the private sector and those run by the city-owned *İETT*. You can differentiate these two types by their colors. Privately run buses are blue-green with yellow non-electronic destination signs while *İETT*-run buses come in many flavors including old red-blue ones, newer green ones and red double-deckers. Tickets that can be obtained in kiosks near bus stops for 1.40 TL are valid only on *İETT* buses and cash payment only on private buses, although if you get on an *İETT* bus the driver will normally accept cash (normally 1.50 TL but this is dependent entirely upon what the driver wishes to charge) and hand you his *Istanbulkart* for you to use.

Recently installed *Metrobüs*, long hybrid buses running on their special lanes separated from all other traffic and thus saving lots of time in Istanbul's usually congested roads, connect western suburb of Avcılar with Kadıköy in Asian Side via Bakırköy, Cevizlibağ which is just out of old city walls near Topkapı Gate, and Mecidiyeköy.

Most bus lines operate between 6AM and around midnight, usually with a reduced volume of services after 10PM. Some lines between major centres operate 24 hr, though, as is the *Metrobüs*, with about an hour intervals. After midnight, buses cost two tickets pp rather than the usual one. Buses and streetcars tend to be very crowded during rush hours, especially on Mondays and Fridays. That can also create opportunities for pickpockets.

24 hr Bus Lines:

- 73 Taksim Square-Ataturk International Airport
- 110 Taksim Square-Kadikoy
- 112 Taksim Square-Bostanci
- 25T Taksim Square-Sariyer
- 40 Taksim Square-Sariyer
- 89C Taksim Square-Basaksehir

- E10 Kadikoy-Sabiha Gokcen International Airport
- 15F Kadikoy-Uskudar
- 130 Kadikoy-Tuzla
- 34A Sogutlucesme(Kadikoy)-Edirnekapi (Metrobus)
- 34 Avcilar-Zincirlikuyu (Metrobus)

As a tourist, you are most likely to use the tram and the metro in the Sultanahmet and Taksim area since there are no bus lines operating in the Sultanahmet area anymore.

By metro

Istanbul's first underground system dates back to 19th century, when the funicular subway "Tünel" was constructed to operate from Karaköy to Istiklal Street in 1875. The distance travelled was 573 metres. This is a good way to go up the hill from the Beyoğlu side of the Galata Bridge to the famous Istiklal Caddesi pedestrian street.

Starting in the 1990's, a modern and extensive (and often confusing) light rail system has been constructed in all parts of the city. The newest (as of October 2014) addition is the Marmaray undersea tunnel, which crosses below the Bosphorus from the the Sultanahmet area to the Anatolian side. Underground lines are called "metro," above ground lines are called "tram," and there are also short, uphill lines called "fünikület," two tiny "teleferik" lines, and the undersea Marmaray. There is also a high-speed bus called Metrobüs, complementary to this whole network.

There are four Metro lines, the first of which has two branches. The most useful to most tourists will be M1A which visits both Atatürk Airport and the Otogar Bus Station, and the M2 which passes near to Sultanahmet and travels to Galata/Taksim and beyond.

All lines are still being extended, but as of October 2014, they include:

- ✓ M1A starts in Aksaray (west of Sultanahmet) and ends at Atatürk Airport, traveling via Emniyet-Fatih, Topkapı-Ulubatlı, Bayrampaşa-Maltepe, Sağmalcılar, Kocatepe, Otogar, Terazidere, Davutpaşa-YTÜ, Merter, Zeytinburnu, Bakırköy-İncirli, Bahçelievler, Ataköy-Şirinevler, Yenibosna, DTM İstanbul Fuar Merkezi, and finally Atatürk International Airport (Havalimanı)

- ✓ M1B also starts in Aksaray and has the same stops as M1A until Otogar. After Otogar, it continues with Esenler, Menderes, Üçyüzlü, and ends Bağcılar Meydan.

- ✓ M2 travels between Yenikapı (south of Sultanahmet) and Hacıosman, stopping at Vezneciler, Haliç, Şişhane (near Galata Tower), Taksim Square (north end of Beyoğlu), Osmanbey, Şişli-Mecidiyeköy, Gayrettepe,

Levent, 4 Levent, Sanayi, İTÜ Ayazağa, Atatürk Oto Sanayi, Darüşşafaka, and finally Hacıosman.

- ✓ M3 is the Kirazlı-Olimpiyat-Başakşehir line. All stops are in the far west of the European side, and therefore unlikely to be of use to tourists and visitors.

- ✓ M4 goes from Kadıköy to Kartal on the Anatolian side, stopping at Ayrılık Çeşmesi, Acıbadem, Ünalan (aka Uzunçayır), Göztepe, Yenisahra, Kozyatağı, Bostancı, Küçükyalı, Maltepe, Huzurevi, Gülsuyu, Esenkent, Hastane-Adliye, Soğanlık, and finally Kartal.

There is also a funicular system connecting Taksim to Kabataş, where you can take ferries across the Bosphorus to the Anatolian side, and also transfer to trams bound for the old city (see below). Another funicular, called Tünel, connects Şişhane to Karaköy (the eastern side of the Galata Bridge).

Nowadays, most metro stations do *not* have a staffed ticket booth, so you will have to obtain your token from automatic token dispensers (called Jetonmatic). Insert coins (except 1 or 5 kuruş) up to 4 TL and then press the button marked *onay* (Turkish for "approval", no English translations are given on all the machines).

A token costs 4 TL (around €1.30) on any urban rail in Istanbul.

By tram

Istanbul Metro & Tram

A tram (line # T1) connects Zeytinburnu (connection to the metro line to the airport) to Kabataş (connection to the underground funicular to Taksim). The line is 14km long, has 24 stations and serves many popular tourist sites (e.g. in Sultanahmet) and ferries (e.g. Eminönü). An entire trip takes 42 minutes.

There are two tram lines running on the same tracks, the line numbered as 38 in front of tram cars runs along the entire T1 line between Kabataş and Zeytinburnu, while significantly shorter line #47 runs between Eminönü and Cevizlibağ stations (the latter of which is abbreviated as C.bağ-A.Ö.Y. on the signage of tram cars). However, both lines call at stations that are of most interest to travellers through the Old City. During morning and evening rush hours every alternate tram runs as #47, while during the rest of the day, most run as #38.

The tram was put in service in 1992 on standard gauge track with modern cars, connecting Sirkeci with Topkapi. The line was extended on one end from Topkapi to Zeytinburnu in March 1994 and, on the other end from Sirkeci to Eminönü in April 1996. On January 30, 2005 it was extended from Sirkeci to Kabataş crossing Golden Horn after 44 years again. 55 vehicles built by ABB run on the line. The daily transport capacity is 155,000 passengers.

Tramway stations are: Zeytinburnu, Mithatpaşa, Akşemsettin, Seyitnizam, Merkezefendi, Cevizlibağ, Topkapı, Pazartekke, Çapa, Fındıkzade, Haseki, Yusufpaşa, Aksaray, Laleli (Üniversite), Beyazıt (Kapalıçarşı), Çemberlitaş, Sultanahmet, Gülhane,

Sirkeci, Eminönü (ferryboats), Karaköy, Tophane, Fındıklı, Kabataş.

Between Taksim and Kabatas, there is a modern underground funicular to connect this tram line to the Taksim metro. The tram is also connected to the southern metro line (for the *Otogar* and Ataturk Airport) at Aksaray station, though the metro and tram lines are a short walk from each other.

During morning and evening rush hours (roughly between 7AM-9AM and 5PM-7:30PM respectively), tram cars run jam-packed so if you intend to take it for a couple of stations down the way, don't even bother walking instead is not only less tiresome than standing in what is essentially more crowded than a sardine can, it's also quicker as you will most likely be able to get in the second or even third tram calling at the station due to the crowd.

There are also two other tram lines linking residential and industrial suburbs in the northwest with the city centre: T2, which heads for Bağcılar, and T4(which is more like *metro-tram* systems of northwestern Europe, as it lies underground for part of its route), which heads for Sultançiftliği, connecting to the Zeytinburnu and Topkapı stations of the T1 line respectively. However, these lines are of very little, if any, use to the average traveller.

Information for disabled travellers
Buses

The process of replacing old buses with newer ones accessible for people using a wheelchair is ongoing. Many buses on central lines have a low floor and a built-in ramp (consult the driver to lean the bus down nearer to the ground, to open the ramp, and to assist into the bus, though any of these might unfortunately be impossible during peak hours in interval stops. Think of a sardine-packed bus unloading all of its passengers to lean down).

By September 2011 LCD screens showing the stop names while approaching to the stop, and voice announcement is made.

Trams
Trams are accessible for people using a wheelchair from the station platforms if you can manage to get into the station in the first place. Some of the stations are located in the middle of very wide avenues and the only access to them is via underground passages (tens of stairs) or overpasses (more stairs!). Otherwise, platforms in tram stations are low and equipped with gentle ramps right from the street (or sidewalk) level. Moda Tramvay and Nostaljik Tramvay run older cars which are not wheelchair-accessible.

All stations are announced both on a display and by voice in the trams.

Metro
All stations and trains in the northern metro line are accessible for people using a wheelchair. Look around the station entrances for handicapped lifts/elevators.

Only some of the stations in the southern metro line are equipped with such elevators (among the stations which have elevators are Aksaray-the main station of the city centre, Otogar-the main bus station, and Havalimanı (Airport) station), but whether there is an elevator or not, if you manage to get into the station (there is a good chance that you can do with a little assistance because the stations in the southern line aren't located as deep as the stations of the northern line are; only about one floor's height under the ground), all trains are accessible from the station platforms, though a little assistance more will be helpful for passing over the narrow gap between the train and the platform. You can ask the guys in grey/black uniforms (security guards, they can be seen in the entrances of the station platforms if not elsewhere) for assistance, it's their duty.

All stations are announced by voice in the metro trains. In northern line it is also announced on a display, but not in the southern line. Instead, you should look at the signs in the stations, which are big and common enough.

By boat

Unique Istanbul liners (large conventional ferry boats), sea-buses (high speed catamarans), or mid-sized private ferries travel between the European and Asian sides of the city. The crossing takes about 20 minutes and costs 1.50 TL, and gives great views of the Bosphorus. *Be aware that sometimes the ferry when arriving at a dock can bounce off the pier accidentally, even on calm days. This can cause people to fall over if they are standing up, so it is advisable to remain seated until the ferry has come to an absolute stop.*

In Istanbul, liners from any given quay generally take only a certain route, and these quays are signposted 'X Iskelesi' ("X Landing stage/pier"). For instance, Eminönü alone has more than 5 landing stages (including the ones used by other ferries apart from liners), so if you should head for, say, Üsküdar, you should take the ferry which departs from 'Üsküdar

Iskelesi'. Replace 'Üsküdar' with the destination of your choice.

Istanbul liners travel on the following routes:

- Karaköy - Haydarpaşa - Kadıköy
- Kadıköy - Eminönü
- Üsküdar - Eminönü
- Üsküdar - Karaköy - Eminönü - Eyüp (The Golden Horn Route)
- Kadıköy - Besiktaş
- Kabatas - Uskudar - Harem
- Istinye - Emirgan - Kanlıca - Anadolu Hisarı - Kandilli - Bebek - Arnavutköy - Çengelköy (The Whole Bosphorus Route)
- Anadolu Kavağı - Rumeli Kavağı - Sariyer
- Eminönü - Kavaklar (Special Bosphorus Tour- Recommended for Tourists)
- Sirkeci - Adalar - Yalova - Cınarcık (The Princes' Islands Route)

Furthermore, the sea-buses (*deniz otobüsü*) follow the same (or more) routes, usually much faster than liners. Returning to Yenikapi from Kadikoy by sea-bus is a fast and convenient way to cross the Bosphorus; at Yenikapi there is a railway station with frequent trains to Sirkeci/Eminönü and the Yenikapi fish restaurant area is close by (or one stop on the train).

Four main private ferry routes for travelling between Asia and Europe sides are:

- Besiktaş - Üsküdar
- Kabataş - Üsküdar *(close to tram and funicular system in Kabataş)*
- Eminönü - Üsküdar *(close to tram in Eminönü)*
- Eminönü - Kadıköy *(close to tram in Eminönü)*

Very useful are the fast ferryboats (travelling at 55 kilometers) running from several points, such as the Yenikapi - Yalova one, that allows you (with a connecting bus in Yalova) to be in Bursa centre in less than three hours. Prices are marginally higher and the gain in time is considerable, though the view is not as nice.

All of the ferries, including private ones, can be paid for using the *AKBIL* system or the new Smart RFID Card that is in the process of introduction.

A new metro line extension crossing the Bosphorus in a tunnel is under construction. This will change the ferry provision and is perhaps a good reason to visit Istanbul before it is completed.

By train
Suburban/commuter trains (*banliyö treni*) using somewhat dilapidated stock and running on national rail network, connect suburbs along the European and Asian coast of the Sea of Marmara to main stations at Sirkeci and Haydarpaşa, respectively. These trains are one of the fastest connections between the old city and western suburbs, especially Bakırköy, although they, especially the line on European Side, are best avoided late at night.

By taxi
Taxis are an easy and cheap way to get around. As of September 2016, start off rate is 3.40 TL (€1.1) and then 2.1 TL (€0.6) for each km afterwards. A one-way travel from Taksim Square to Sultanahmet costs approximately 10-15 TL. Tipping is generally unnecessary. Occasionally, drivers will refuse to start the meter and try to negotiate a fixed price (but most drivers will start taximeters at all times). You should avoid these cabs and simply take another one as you will almost certainly end paying too much. To be sure, before getting in, just ask "how much to go to ...?" (most of the drivers understand basic English) since the price they tell then is quite accurate. Tell them then to put the taximeter on. Drivers do normally work with the taximeter, so they will not be surprised at all when you ask them to put it on. The price at the end will be quite close to the one they tell you at the beginning. There is now, as of October 2009, just one fare unit, it means, there is no extra fare at night.

Taxis that wait near a bus station are usually a tourist trap. They start the meter but charge you 20 TL at least. Emphasize to the driver that you will pay for the meter price before getting in. Do not buy their quick-sell tricks. Always try to stop a taxi that is passing by on the road or find a legitimate taxi stop.

Insist on going to the destination that you want because some drivers are payed by commission for each time they have someone go to a certain site.

Beware riding a taxi other than the "yellow-colored" ones since the other-colored taxis are registered under different cities and have a different rating system.

Be careful on what notes you hand them for payment; some drivers have tried to pretend that the 50 lira note that was handed was just a 5 lira note. Occasionally taxi drivers may actually also rip notes you give them, and tell you it is no good, in order to make you hand them a 50 lira note. So, make sure the notes are not ripped, and is actually the right one before you hand them over. Also, if you are not familiar with the city the taxi driver may drive a detour in order to charge you more.

Traffic can be very bad, it can take an hour for a few km through the old city. You might be better off taking the metro out of the old city and then a taxi from there.

Some important routes with distances and estimated taxi fares are :

- Ataturk Airport (IST) - Taxim Square ~ 21 km.
- Ataturk Airport (IST) - Sultanahmet Square (Old City) ~ 18 km.
- Taxim Square - Sultanahmet (Old City) ~ 5,5 km.
- Sabiha Gokcen Airport (SAW) - Kadikoy (Chalcadonia) Ferry Terminal ~ 36 km.
- Esenler (Bus Terminal) - Topkapi Palace (Sultanahmet) ~ 10,5 km.
- Esenler (Bus Terminal) - Ataturk Airport (IST) ~ 15 km.

By shared taxi
Dolmuş (Turkish: "full") is a shared taxi, travelling on a fixed route, which costs more than a city autobus but less than a normal taxi. They can carry up to 8 passengers. They are easy to recognize, because they also have the yellow painting as taxis and carry a *Dolmus* sign on its top. They will only start driving when all eight places are filled, which is also where the name derives from.

The main and most important routes for Dolmuses are :

- ➢ Taksim - Eminönü (Taksim stop, near the Ataturk Cultural Center, in Taksim square)
- ➢ Taksim - Kadıköy
- ➢ Taksim - Bostanci
- ➢ Taksim - Aksaray (Taksim stop, Tarlabasi Avenue, close to Taksim square)
- ➢ Kadıköy - Bostanci (Bostanci stop, in front of the Bostanci ferry port)

- Taksim - Tesvikiye (Taksim stop, in front of Patisserie Gezi, in Taksim square)
- Beşiktaş - Nisantasi (Beşiktaş stop, in front of the Beşiktaş - Üsküdar ferry port)
- Kadıköy - Üsküdar (Üsküdar stop, Near the Üsküdar - Beşiktaş and Üsküdar - Kabataş ferry port)

If you want the driver to make a stop, you can say İnecek var. (EE-neh-djek war!) (Someone's getting out.) or Müsait bir yerde. (mU-sa-EEt bir yer-deh.) (At a convenient spot.).

Things to Do in Istanbul

Istanbul is hustling, beautiful, busy, chaotic, romantic, historic, kitsch, gorgeous depending on which part of the city you are and the time of day. A city of over 14 million people the time of day really would change the impression you get from where you are at. People move in this vast city built on two continents crossing continents, covering huge distances within the city.

You may still relax, take your time and enjoy as long as you go to the right places at the right times. Want to relax? Then hit a side street, take a boat cruise, sit at a cafe on the Bosphorus, immerse yourself in Byzantine times in the quiet of a mosaic museum or watch the beautiful tiles in Blue Mosque. Want to see some city rush and human touch? Then go to Istiklal Street and just watch people pass by.

European side is the business side, Asian the residential. Most people who work at foreign and domestic major corporations have left the city center for a life in the far suburbs where big gated communities, or even small scale cities in peripheries of Istanbul and are commuting daily to the city center. But they sure are missing the center!

Where ever you go, one thing is for sure: there's something strange about this city. May be it is because it has seen three empires in its long history: East Roman, Byzantine and Ottoman Empires. May be it has seen so many kinds of people from different parts of the world: Europe, Middle East, Central Asia, Eurasia, Africa.. Or may be it is just this strange mix that it offers. A blend of east and west or a fusion of old and new or a combination of traditional and modern. Is Istanbul the furthest east of the west? Or is it just the other way around? Are Turks eastern or western? Is "contrast" an Istanbul born phenomenon?

You have to see it yourself and decide. The Vikings named it Miklagard "big city", the Slavs called it Tsarigrad, "City of Caesar", for the Greeks it has been Konstantinapolis. May be you will have a name of your own for Istanbul once you get to see this place. The thing is: you have to see this place

Places to See in Istanbul

Old Town

Topkapi Palace
Topkapi Palace is the symbol and the center of the Ottoman Empire. Overlooking Istanbul Bogazici (Bosphorus) and the Marmara sea, stands this amazing

building that was the great palace of the Ottoman Sultans. The palace is a collection of buildings arranged around a series of courtyards and has incredible collections of jewels, China, pieces of Ottoman and Islamic artwork.

Saint Sophie
Saint Sophie, built by Constantin the Great, also known as the church of the Divine Wisdom was designed to show the strength and wealth of the Roman emperors. Once it was the greatest Christian church in the world.

Sultanahmet Mosque (The Blue Mosque)
Sultanahmet Mosque (Blue Mosque), in Turkish Sultanahmet Camii, is known as the Blue Mosque, because of its magnificient interior decorations of blue Iznik tiles. Outside of the mosque stands the turbe or the tomb of Sultan Ahmet. It is decorated with 17th century Iznik tiles. The Sultan was buried here along with his wife and three sons.

Hippodrome

Hippodrome, the arena with the scenes of chariot races and also cultural focus of the Byzantine (Roman) Empire. Remains of the three of the great monuments can be seen: the Obelisk of Theodosius, the bronze Serpentine Column and the Column of Constantine. The square, with its surroundings, is like an open-air museum.

Underground Cistern -Yerebatan Sarayi
Basilica Cistern, built in the fourth century, is one of the underground cisterns that riddle the foundations of the city. It has been extensively excavated and renovated and is worth visiting and exploring while listening to the tunes of classical music. A unique experience !

Archeological Museum
Archeological Museums This is in close vicinity of Topkapi Palace, in the direction of Gulhane park entrance. There are many collections in the museum. From Egyptian and Assyrian empires to Roman and Byzantine statues, marvellous sarchophagi, and pieces

of Temples. The rich collection of ancient art are brought from anicent sites all over Anatolia (Turkey).

Suleymaniye Camii
Suleymaniye Mosque built by Mimar Sinan, the great architect, and completed in just seven years is considered to be the most beautiful of all Imperial mosques in Istanbul. It dominates the skyline of the Golden Horn. Adjoining the mosque there are schools of theology, schools of Medicine, and a caravanserai.

Dolmabahce Palace
Dolmabahce Palace was built as a second residence to the Sultan Abdulmecid mid 19th century. The palace commands a nice view right on the Bosphorus and its gardens are very pretty, especially in spring and summer. The founder of Turkey, Mustafa Kemal Ataturk has died in this palace on November 10, 1938 at 9.05 AM.

Grand Bazaar
Grand Bazaar, the world's biggest covered historic Bazaar. It is one of the most famous spots of Istanbul,

always filled with crowds who not only come to shop but to window-shop carpets, jewellery, leathers, handcrafts, home decoration items and many more.

Galata Tower
Galata Tower is located in the Galata area of Beyoglu district. Galata tower is one the best vista points in Istanbul with sweeping views of Istanbul including the Golden Horn.

The Museum of Turkish Islamic Art
Turkish and Islamic Arts Museum was the Palace of Ibrahim Pasa, now is a museum containing a large collection of Islamic artwork.

Beylerbeyi Palace
Beylerbeyi Palace is located on the Asian side of the Bosphorus slightly to the north of Dolmabahce Palace, right under the first bridge which connects Asia and Europe. Much smaller in size, the palace is a nice example of Ottoman architecture.

Chora Church

Chora Church, known also as St. Saviour, this church is famous for its mosaics. The second most important Byzantine church in Istanbul, has beautiful frescoes with the theme of death and resurrection.

Rustem Pasa Mosque
Rustem Pasha Mosque, a 16th century Ottoman Mosque which is known to have the best examples of handmade Iznik tiles, not only inside but outside the mosque as well.

Spice Market
Spice Market is a small bazaar, known in Turkish as Misir (Epgyptian) bazaar. As the name suggests,the shops have hunderds if not thousands of different spices and different types of food,from caviars to pistachios.

Rumeli Fortress
Rumeli Fortress The fortress is located on the Boshorus. It was built by the Ottomans before the conquest of Istanbul. Most of the walls are restored and is one of the hightlights of a Bosphorus cruise.

Restaurants

Nightlife

Istanbul Nightlife: There are shows which does include folkloric shows, as well as belly dancing, in several clubs whose clientele are foreign tourists. Nightlife Turkish people are used to consist of bars and discos which are mostly similar to the ones found in Western countries. However, they have major differences in terms of clientele and atmosphere and sometimes the music played.

You can get a feel of the Turkish nightlife in Beyoglu, on Istiklal street. There are many bars in the region almost all on side streets, most of them being within only around 100 feet from the main street.

Ortakoy, another bar and nightlife district, is a much smaller place but more densely populated with bars, as well artisans selling their handicrafts on the streets daytime or nighttime.

Things to do in Istanbul

Things to do in Istanbul depends on your vacation time in Istanbul. Places to see in Istanbul offers a list of major sights in Istanbul.

The absolutely must see places would be Topkapi Museum, Hagia Sophia and Blue Mosque. They are very close to each other, 5 minutes walking distance apart in Sultanahmet area.

You may also get travel ideas in many sections of Istanbul Guide especially under Sightseeing Locations header as well as in Istanbul Travel Tips

Once you have visited major sights in the Old Town and Beyoglu area and have taken a boat along the Bosphorus, there are still many other things to do.

Istanbul Archeological Museum is possibly the most overlooked museum in Istanbul. There you will find pieces from ancient sites around Turkey including sarcophagus of Alexander. The cafe of this museum is gorgeous as the shades offer great relief from the Istanbul sun and you would be surrounded by ancient

Greek and Roman artwork in the beautiful garden. So while strolling down at the exit of Topkapi Museum just pass through Haghia Irini (St. Irene) church and walk a minute to reach the museum's garden. The museum has great ancient pieces brought from around Turkey.

Visit to a Turkish Bath is not an unusual thing to do. There are two major baths one is in Sultanahmet and the other is in Galatasaray which have been catering to tourists since a long time.

Istanbul Views

Istanbul is a city of fascinating views. Whether you are a photographer or not, check locations with great Istanbul views.

Try a cafe in Bebek. If you would like to the see of the campus of the best Turkish University with incredible vistas over the Bosphorus then visit Bogazici University, an ex-American college. Enter through Rumelihisari gate and get out from the Bebek gate. Bosphorus is Bogazici in English.

Beaches

There are no spectular beaches like the ones you can find in the Southern or Western Turkey. However if you have plenty of time in your hands and are curious enough to travel about more than an hour, you may head to beach clubs in Kilyos area. Alternatively, you may visit Caddebostan on the Asian side. From May till September you may check Caddebostan beach, you will just see a waterfront upscale neighboorhood a walkway, a beach, skaters, joggers, all you can find at your home town. At the same time you can see regular Istanbul people . There are two small, overcrowded beaches along with a private posh club pierr.

Sultanahmet Travel Guide

Sultanahmet is famous for its meatballs. That and the magnificient Hagia Sophia church, Topkapi Palacecommanding the Bosphorus and the amazingly beautiful Blue Mosque. And the Hippodrome, Basilica Cistern, Archeology Museum, Great Palace Mosaic

Museum and the carpet salesmen though their numbers are decreasing. It is extremely multinational, beautiful with its gardens and open spaces, easy with its cafes, relaxing under the shade of the trees decorating its side streets. And then busy again with bus loads of tourists. Sultanahmet is both part of Istanbul and the whole world.

In the 1960s not many tourists came. And those who visited the city were the hippies mostly from Europe and the US, They stayed in cheap dirty hotel rooms, were fed free by caring restaurant owners and they smoked. That was like 1960's everywhere in the West, Sultanahmet was the place of the West at those times. Istanbul residents avoided Sultanahmet.

In 1963 James Bond (Sean Connery) came to Istanbul with the now classic With Love From Russia. It was that same year after starting "nouveau roman" movement in France, Alain Robbe Grillet came to Istanbul to shoot his beautiful "L'Immortelle". What a wonderful experience to see Istanbul in old movies as so much has changed since then.

And there was a Sultanahmet prison where most famous socialist political prisoners and some of the greatest figures of not only of Turkish literature but also the world literature like Nazim Hikmet were held. Nowadays that prison is converted to a luxury international hotel.

Times have sure changed but Sultanahmet is as beautiful as always. You can stay here to immerse yourself in history or to avoid tourists you can stay elsewhere in Istanbul and visit during day time. It depends absolutely how tourist intolerant you are but Sultanahmet surely is one of the best places to stay in Istanbul.

Turkish and Islamic Arts Museum

Turkish and Islamic Arts Museum is a museum located in Sultanahmet Square, just opposite of Blue Mosque. At first the museum building was the palace of Ibrahim

Pasha, who was the first grand vizier to Suleyman the Magnificent. After the proclamation of the Turkish Republic, it started to serve as a museum.

Turkish and Islamic Arts Museum is the first museum covering the Turkish and Islamic art collections in Turkey. Its major sections are Wood Works Department, Department of Ethnography, Stone Art Section, Department of Ceramic and Glass, Metal Art Department, Department of Carpet and Department of Manuscripts and Calligraphy.

These exhibitions display Turkish history, ranging from earlier periods beginning in the 8th century, Seljuk (11th to 13th centuries) to the Ottoman (14th to 20th centuries). Especially, Carpet Department is unique with Selcuk carpets.

In addition, it has a court where you can relax and drink Turkish coffee with the view of Sultanahmet, Hagia Sophia and Topkapi Palace.

The museum is open between the hours of 8.00am-5.30pm everyday except monday. Entrance fee is 5 tl (~2 euro) per person.

Taksim Travel Guide

If you are looking for a city center in this vast city running a coastline of tens of kilometers in both Asia and Europe, that would be Taksim. It is the hub of the city. All major transportation lines except ferries go through this point and you can reach ferry connection from Taksim in only 3 minutes ride on the new funiculare running down to Kabatas.

Yes, there are other central points or city nodes such as Besiktas, Aksaray, Mecidiyekoy and Bakirkoy on the European side and Kadikoy, Uskudar on the Asian side but Taksim is the heart of the city.

Taksim's landmark for Turkish people is AKM, short for Ataturk Cultural Center, a period building which is not interesting or beautiful as a building but has the biggest significance in the cultural life of Istanbul and

Turkey in classical music, opera and ballet. It is the building that much symbolizes the direction of Turkey under Ataturk's principles, to be on par with Western nations not only in economy but in culture. Many of the Istanbul Festivals and Events were held here. It signifies a young Turkish State's move towards the culture of the West. The architecture reflects functionality rather than beauty, something you would expect as the Turkish Ataturkist State with limited funds wanted to provide a place for Istanbul citizens to connect with art and artists. In addition to music shows and concerts many art exhibitions were held here. That did really worked and great artist from around the world came to play as well as the young and established Turkish artists. Nowadays it still is a landmark building but there are many new venues and concert halls in Istanbul.

The monument which has a special significance in Turkish people's daily political lives is located on Taksim Square. This is the Ataturk's statue. Public figures, political parties and NGO's lay wreath here to salute and protect the memory and ideals of Mustafa Kemal Ataturk and the secular state he has founded.

When you speak of Taksim, a Turk would think of Beyoglu and Istiklal street though Taksim is the Taksim square and immediate area around. Taksim extends to the other side in the direction of Elmadag, Harbiye and posh Nisantasi nerighborhhood, but in the mind of Turks Taksim means mosty Beyoglu. For travelers and Istanbullus alike, Taksim and Beyoglu, area is the place for shopping for antiques, old maps, old books, stamps, dining, partying and people watching.

Beyoglu Travel Guide

Beyoglu is where Istanbul's shopping, looking, eating, entertaining heart beats. It is a busy neighborhood day and night, cosmopolitan and at times chaotic. This is where you can find great food at decent prices, cheap beers as well as expensive dinners. It is also cultural heart of the city with movie theaters, art galleries and museums including the Pera Museum, the most important in Beyoglu and among top museums in Istanbul.

The ever crowded Istiklal street crosses Beyoglu from Tunel, Asmalimescit neighborhoods to Taksim Square and is what comes to people's mind first when they think of Beyoglu. A nostalgic tram crosses Istiklal Street but it is better to walk. The side streets just off Istiklal street offer pleasant surprises whether for art, food or drinks and waiting to be discovered.

History of Beyoglu
Beyoglu, also known as Pera district, is part of Galata, a trade colony of the Genoese and the Venetians formed during the Byzantine times.

After the conquest of Istanbul in 1453, the colony continued its existence under Ottoman rule. The transformation of this region into a wealthy Western oriented district happened in mid 19th century. It was where wealthy foreigners, ambassadors, influential Jewish, Armenian and Greek minorities lived. It was the finance capital of the Ottoman Empire, not unlike Wall Street of those times. Neoclassical and art nouveau buildings are a testimony of that period.

After the founding of the Turkish Republic, it lost importance as a financial and influential district in state affairs but it has kept its distinct Western feel and the symbol of the West in the eyes of Istanbul residents. Hence until the 1950's Taksim and Beyoglu were a special district for the Turkish people too.

That all changed with the influx of rural people immigrating to Istanbul from around Turkey who were building slums in the peripheries of the city after Wall Street backed right wing party has promised to create immediate wealth for everyone. Unfortunately, that promise happened to be mostly by land speculation as opposed to the period of Ataturk when wealth was generated through labour and production. To date 60% of the city is still made of illegal or once illegal but later transformed to legal buildings by politicians. These buildings are called gecekondus and they still are an ongoing concern in Istanbul.

The only major place these slum people were able to take a hold in Istanbul city center was Beyoglu, so the region was inundated with poor young people with no jobs. Needless to say crime had flourished in the 70s and 80s and although contained in recent years it still goes on in the boundaries of the Beyoglu, along with some notorious bars.

Things to Do in Beyoglu
Spend some time whether in a small passage cafe off Istiklal or head for shopping, food, entertainment. The population of Beyoglu has changed after Istiklal street was converted to a pedestrian street in 1990 and the arrival of Turkish and foreign highly educated, well paid people. The first people to settle in the neighborhood after Istiklal street changes were artists, professors and bohemes. Later on came business, then big business and finally high end shops. Nowadays it is the cosmopolitan lively district of Istanbul. Most buildings

have been renovated, upper class restaurants and bars have flourished and the side streets became multicultural, not much unlike a piece of NYC with hip new cafes, bars and restaurants springing up monthly.

Today Beyoglu area is the place for shopping for antiques, old maps, old books, stamps, fine dining, partying and people watching. There are four districts worth mentioning in Beyoglu area, Asmalimescit, Cihangir, Galata and Cukurcuma. Tarlabasi is a rundown neighborhood you should avoid, as it is notorious for criminals.

Galata Tower and the Galata Whirling Dervish Hall (Galata Mevlevihanesi) are the most important historic landmarks of Beyoglu district.

How to Go to Beyoglu
Walking from Taksim on Istiklal Street or walking up the Galip Dede/Yuksek Kaldirim street from Karakoy or simply taking the tunel (one stop metro) from Karakoy.

Galata Istanbul

Galata is where Geonese trade colony representing Republic of Genoa in Italy was settled in 1273 under the reign of Byzance until the conquest of Istanbul in 1453. Galata is the hillside area between the Tunel end of Istiklal street and Karakoy. Galata is part of Beyoglu district municipally but the name Beyoglu(Pera District) refers to the area around Istiklal street from Taksim to Tunel.

The landmark building of Galata neighborhood is Galata Tower. It offers sweeping 360 degrees views of Istanbul including Halic (Golden Horn).

Galata neighborhood is home to NeoBaroque and NeoRenaissance style buildings in Istanbul particularly around Bankalar Caddesi (Wall Street of Ottoman Empire). If you walk from Karakoy up the hill to Galata tower there are three parallel streets. One is the obivious and direct route that is busy with tourists and Istanbul residents.

The other two are parallel side street (one with Camondo stairs with a sign for Austrian Hospital, Avurturya Hastanesi) climbs which originate a hundred meters or so up the Bankalar Caddesi. To arrive Galata tower from a side street such as Camekan street is even more impressive. Along the uphill walk you will also see cafes with nice views of Bosphorus.

Kuledibi Goz Hastanesi (Kuledibi Eyecare Hospital) is an interesting historic building which will be converted to a museum. It was built by British artchitect for quarantine hospital of British sailors. When traveling from Kadikoy to Karakoy or vice versa from sea you will notice this building right under Galata tower. It looks like a castle and somehow out of place for Istanbul. You cannot visit indoors but just looking from outside it is an interesting sight.

Galata was home to Galata Stock Exchange (started in 1865) during the Ottoman period when capitulations where given to bankers and corporations. Bank buildings in the area in Karakoy Bankalar Caddesi date back to late 1800s.

What to Do in Galata
Use side streets of Galata in day time. At night only use well lit preferably crowded Galata streets. There are many art galeries around Galata It is a nice experience to immerse oneself in historic narrow streets of Galata.

In some streets in Galata, around the Galata tower, you will see luxury designer apparel shops, cafes, gift shops, sweet shops and bakeries. The neighborhood is being transformed from being a run down neighborhood since 1950s to a hip one, a bit like Greenwich village transformation in NewYork from the 1980s to 2000s.

How to Go to Galata
Walk to and around Galata either starting at sea level Karakoy or Tunel end which is also the end of Istiklal street coming from Taksim.

Bosphorus

Bosphorus is the name of the straights that separate Asia and Europe. It looks like a wide river flowing from the Black Sea to the Marmara Sea. It is fairly recent, dating to about 5600 BC. With new discoveries of neolithic settlements in Istanbul dating back to 6400 BC we now know that people actually walked from Asia to Europe back then.

Bosphorus is very important for trade and political strategy and has been the target of foreign empires throughout history. Gallipoli War was an attempt by the British Empire to cross Canakkale (Dardanelles) straights and then control Bosphorus and Istanbul. After Ottoman Empire lost the war along with its ally Germany in WWI, British ships had invaded the Bosphorus in 1918.

Bosphorus is the most important natural beauty of Istanbul. From Kadikoy in the Marmara Sea in the south to Anadolu Kavagi and Poyrazkoy at the Black Sea north the Bosphorus offers visitors a wonderful view of seaside mansions, woods, hills, palaces and mosques. There are many ways to do a Bosphorus Cruise for different budgets and durations. A guided tour would be beneficial to not only indicate the places of interest but also the history behind them.

Anadolu Kavagi, last stop of Bosphorus ferry and Yoros Castle Istanbul

Istanbul by Night, Passenger boats, fish market, bosphorus cruise, Anadolu Kavagi where the Genoese castle up the hill offers views of the Black sea and the Bosphorus. Anadolu kavagi is the last stop of Bosphorus cruise of the Istanbul municipality ferry boats.

Yoros Castle up the hill in Anadolu Kavagi was built by a Genoese trade colony. It also amazing to think that Anadolu Kavagi was also home to Phoenician trade colony, sailors sailing from Lebanon, some 3000 years ago. Recent archeological excavations are done in the castle.

What to Do in Anadolu Kavagi and Yoros Castle

Anadolu Kavagi is a small fishing village north of the Bosphorus on the Asian side where you can have lunch. You may eat fried mussle sandwitches if you are into seafood especially good during winter and spring time. You should do the bargaining for the fish before you enter any fish restaurant. There are also many waffle shops and fast food places around the boat station.

You can do a short trek above the small fishing village to the Genoese Yoros Castle overlooking the Black sea and the Bosphorus. The vistas are wonderful, in a blue sea extending over to Odessa, Ukraine. You will see ships going to countries around black Sea such as Ukraine, Russia, Bulgaria, Romania and Georgia. They look like small whitish dots on the blue of the sea. And if you turn around you will see the straight of Bosphorus in all its grandeur lying to the south.

How to Go to Anadolu Kavagi and Yoros Castle
Anadolu Kavagi is the last stop of municipality ferries departing Eminonu. Please note that most other Bopshorus cruises and tours do not travel as far as

Anadolu Kavagi. Inquire before joining a cruise as Anadolu Kavagi is close to the end of Black Sea entrance of Bopshorus and far from Eminonu or Besiktas.

Prince's Islands Istanbul

Starting in spring but especially during summer months, Prince's Islands are a piece of Mediterranean life in Istanbul. They are a group of islands close to the shores of Istanbul. Of this island group four of the bigger are Buyukada (biggest), Heybeliada, Kinaliada and Burgaz.

Buyukada is the biggest one of the Princes' Islands, the others being Kinaliada, Burgazada, Sedefadasi and Heybeliada. There is no motor vehicle traffic in Buyukada and it seems so far away from the crowds of Istanbul if only you can make it on weekdays. These islands were in fact exile places for the royal Byzantians and now they host gorgeous summer houses, hotels, private clubs, some beaches and restaurants. There are people living on these islands all year long as the ferry service of Istanbul city also cover these Islands although it is less frequent compared to other main lines in Istanbul.

What to Do in Prince's Islands
If you have time to visit only one island, Buyukada it should be. Since the islands are a part of the Greek culture of Istanbul, the main attraction on Buyukada is Ayayorgi (St.George) monastery which stands on top of a hill that takes about half an hour of a hike. You can also get a horse carriage or rent a bicycle in your free time until the end of this tour. There are beaches in both coasts the one facing Istanbul and the other facing towards to Marmara Sea.

In the Islands, you can taste sea food, fried mussels or kokorec. Buyukadasi is suggested over the other islands if you have limited time. You can do a tour of the island with horse buggies.

You can rent a bike, or a horse buggy and do a small tour (kucuk tur) or big tour (buyuk tur) of the Buyukada island.

How to Go to Prince's Islands
You can go the Prince's islands from Eminonu, Kabatas (down from Taksim by funiculaire), Kadikoy and Bostanci, being the closest point to the islands among them. There are seabuses (fast ferries) and regular boats (Sehir hatlari) and also privately operated boats from Bostanci at the same prices as regular boats.

Kadikoy Travel Guide

Kadikoy is center and transportation hub of Asian side of Istanbul. Kadikoy is a port for regular ferries faster ferries (sea buses) and bus, dolmush connections to most locations in Istanbul.

The pretty, intellectual neighborhood of Moda is only 10 minutes walk away and if you take the seaside pedestrian walk from Kadikoy to Moda, you may even feel yourself in a seaside resort at the same time looking at the silhouettes of Topkapi Palace, Blue Mosque St. Sophia in Sultanahmet across the Bosphorus.

Kadikoy is not only the name of the centre where ferries dock but also the name of the district which encompasses neigborhoods along the posh Bagdat Caddesi such as Fenerbahce, Caddebostan, Saskinbakkal, Suadiye along with many inland locations such as Erenkoy, Kozyatagi etc. The seaside strip from Kadikoy to Bostanci is most attractive to visit. There are no historic sights of major importance but bits and pieces of history such as Old Ottoman houses, spread among recently build multistory buildings.

The district is home to the biggest football (soccer) club in Turkey, Fenerbahce whose stadium attracts 60,000 fans to the games. The stadium is about 15 minutes walk from the center of Kadikoy.

Residents of Kadikoy are progressive, though not as multicultural as Beyoglu area. Yet in recent years increasing numbers of travelers from around the world stay in Kadikoy as well as expats and students who stay for long term. Moda especially attracts most foreigners as it is right accross the Bosphorus from Sultanahmet, Kabatas (via metro to Taksim) and Besiktas.

Kadikoy is also home to Haydarpasa Railway Station serving cities around Turkey and some Middle Eastern cities.

Things to Do in Kadikoy
A walk in Kadikoy marketplace (Kadikoy Carsisi in Turkish) is highly suggested though very crowded. Shops that sell fresh fruits and vegeables, cheese, fresh fish as well as bakeries, restaurants and bars crowd the streets of Kadikoy. Kokerec, fried mussels, boreks, simits are cheap and tasty alternatives to full course meals. Travelers from the US and Europe have reported an easygoing, less pushy attitude in the marketplace. There are also many bars and cafes in the area, similar to Beyoglu but smaller in size.

Sureyya Opera house, a historic building, is the only opera building in Istanbul a is located 10 minutes to the center on Bahariye street the equivalent of Istiklal in Beyoglu but shorter and much less crowded. There many theaters and movie theaters in Kadikoy.

How to Go to Kadikoy
There are ferries from many corners of European side of Istanbul at 20-30 minutes intervals, such asEminonu, Karakoy which is across the Galata Bridge from Eminonu, Besiktas. Before boarding the ferry you can also buy simit and share some of it with seagulls that accompany the boats by throwing bits of it in the air. You should be on top deck (mostly modern boats have top decks) or the back of the boat.

Don't forget a ferry ride gives some of most beautiful photo shooting opportunities in Istanbul.

Moda Travel Guide

Moda is one of the best places to live in Istanbul. It is centrally located yet isolated from crowds, located about 10 minutes walking distance from Kadikoy, the center of the Asian side of Istanbul. For travelers it offers a glimpse into a silent residential part of Istanbul with spectacular views across the Bosphorus of the Sultanahmet area, Old Town of Istanbul.

There is a nostalgic tram from Kadikoy but it is easier and faster to walk. It is a modern, progressive neighborhood and getting more popular among foreigners from Europe and US.

Moda is where many Turkish intellectuals, poets, literary figures lived and continue to live. There are many historic buildings in Moda from St. Joseph French High School (1870) to many Ottoman style small houses and Melih Eczanesi on Moda street, a pharmacy founded first in 1902 in another building.

Things to Do in Moda
Famous places are the Moda Tea Garden (Moda Cay bahcesi), Ice Cream of Ali (Ali'nin Dondurmasi), bier garden by the seaside near, not on the dock, the Moda ferry dock which does not receive a regular ferry

service any more. Sureyya Opera House, many movie theaters such as Rexx, restaurants, bars and pubs in the neighborhood provide easy access to entertainment.

Moda is a nice place to visit in summer.

How to Go to Moda
By boat to Kadikoy and a walk 10-15 minute walk. You can either take the seaside route or go inland through Kadikoy market then up to Moda street (Moda Caddesi) and walk all the way down to Moda on that same street.

Halic (Golden Horn) Istanbul, Fener, Balat, Eyup Sutluce

Golden horn (Halic in Turkish) is a cove, a natural harbor serving trade colonies and empires for thousands of years. The Marmara Sea entrance is marked with Galata Bridge between Karakoy and Eminonu. Karakoy is the port area just under the hill of Galata area hence the name Galata Bridge.

Eyup, Fener, Balat neighborhoods are among the historic parts of the Istanbul Old Town along the Golden horn. Greek Orthodox Patriarch, Bulgarian iron cast church, Ottoman style house, Greek Fener High School are major sights of the area. There are good fish restaurants along the Golden horn especially in or near Balat.

Golden horn was extremely polluted due to the existence many factories decades ago but during a 20 year period it has been greatly cleaned so much so that serious amateur fishing takes places on the Galata bridge at the intersection of Golden horn and the Marmara Sea. Some people even catch enough Istavrit (small Marmara sea fish, most tasty when crisp fried) to sell.

Golden horn has a special historical signficance during conquest of Istanbul. Byzance had closed off the Golden horn from the sea by huge chains from one side to the other but Fatih Sultan Mehmet (the Conqeror) had ships moved from the sea over rolling timbers and entered the Golden Horn much to the surprise of the Byzantine emperor.

Bebek Travel Guide

It has always been said that Istanbul is a mixture of East and West. Probably Bebek is among the most Western of this amazing city. Widely touted as one of poshest neighbourhoods of Istanbul, Bebek is located between Rumeli Fortress and Arnavutkoy. However, what really makes this neighborhood special is the existence of the most competitive Turkish university Bogazici University, on top of Bebek hills.

Being a cove on the Boshorus, Bebek is a small natural port. Formerly, it was a little fishing village. Its popularity dates back to the 18th century when people started to built waterside residences. Since that time it has always been an upscale area. In the beginning, its port was used as a port of refuge. Now yachts and boats anchor along the coast.

Another nice thing about Bebek, besides being a charming small village along the Bosphorus is the existence of a hillside small forest which unfortunately has become very rare in Istanbul due to unplanned, looting and squatting style urbanization, especially around the hills along the Bosphorus with the exception of military zones and parks. In the past Istanbul was a very green city with its forests. But now, as an inevitable result of unplanned, looting style urbanization there are much less trees let alone forests. However, Bebek still reserves its beautiful trees.

Life in Bebek is very peaceful and quiet with the exception of the coast where rich kids come to show some of the most expensive cars in the world. Yet the streets and the park is crowded by people from all walks of life who would like to spend some time by the sea.

Things to Do in Bebek

Along the coastal road, lie a row of stylish elegant shops such as patisseries, bookstores and cafes. Some international cafe chains have possibly their most beautiful shops in the world in this neighborhood with terraces right on the sea. It is worth having a coffee in these shops even just for the atmosphere. Taking a walk along the sea and sitting on the second floor of cafes along the sea would be the top thing to do in Bebek.

You can eat tasty cakes, waffles, drink tea or coffee and read your book in these cafes with the lovely view of Bosphorus. For example, 'Bebek Kahvesi' is a ubiquitous example of neighborhood cafes where Bogazici students hang out too, though it does not have the same view as other chain cafes.

In addition Bebek has a vibrant nightlife with bars and restaurants which are always full even in workdays.

Asiyan Mezarligi cemetery of famous Turkish authors such as Orhan Veli down from south campus of

Bogazici University, university campus itself and Bebek Park are among the places worth seeing. Besides Bebek Mosque located to the west of the cove, there is also an Eastern Orthodox Church and a Catholic Church. Probably the most beautiful building of Bebek is the Egyptian consulate mansion right on the Bosphorus.

How to Go to Bebek
You can take buses No 40,42t or 40t from Taksim. Many other buses depart Eminonu and Besiktas The bus ride will be a pleasant ride along the Bosphorus. Or you can take ferries from main districts of Istanbul such as Eminonu and Besiktas. For more information see ferry hours for boats serving the Bosphorus.

Ortakoy Travel Guide

Ortakoy is the first district of Istanbul that would be classified in local usage as part of the Bosphorus on the European side, traveling north towards the Black Sea from the Old Town. In Istanbul talk "going to the Bosphorus" means going away from the central locations located on the Bosphorus such as Kadikoy, Eminonu, Uskudar, Besiktas, Karakoy towards further north for a day by the sea, either for a fish restaurant or a cafe on the sea.

Ortakoy is not only idyllic with tiny little shops, fast food eateries, a small square by the sea but also offers a lot cheaper cafes and restaurants compared to other locations along the Bosphorus even though there are some high end restaurants and bars right on the sea. For these reasons it is very crowded during especially weekends and at summer nights even during weekdays, popular among both locals and tourists. Behind the Ortakoy mosque, boats depart for a one hour or one and a half hour Bosphorus Cruise.

Ortakoy literally means middle village as it was located in the middle of the European side of Bosphorus, before many new villages were built as Istanbul expanded. It is situated on the Bosphorus, between Besiktas and Bebek districts of Istanbul, at about 15 minutes walk from Besiktas.

Things to Do in Ortakoy

During the Ottoman era, Ortakoy hosted many people from different backgrounds. Therefore different religious buildings, mosques, churches, synagogues stand side by side. The most famous of them, theOrtakoy Mosque also known as Grand Imperial Mosque of Sultan Abdülmecid built in the 19th century is really worth seeing with its Neo-Baroque architecture style and is the one that is used in most photo shoots and commercials for Istanbul. It is the only major mosque right on the sea.

There is Ortakoy Square by the sea, famous with its delicious baked jacket potatoes and waffles. On its side streets and the square area there are also many tea and coffee houses where you can sit, read your newspaper and enjoy the magnificent view of the Bosphorus with the sounds of sea gulls.

There are several antique and second hand shops on the side streets of Ortakoy, though more expensive than others.

Ortakoy is also where the columns of the first bridge "Bogazici Koprusu" on the Bosphorus stand. The second being Fatih Sultan Mehmet bridge further up north the Bosphorus over Rumeli Hisari.

In addition, the Turkish Bath built by the famous architect Mimar Sinan can be seen here, but unfortunately, it is not working anymore.

Formerly used as parliament building until the 20th century, today Ciragan Palace serves as one of the most luxurious hotels of Istanbul by the name of Ciragan Palace Kempinski Hotel in Ortakoy.

Ortakoy also has a vivid nightlife. There are many elegant restaurants, cafes and bars also prefered by Turkish celebrities.

How to Go to Ortakoy
Due to its central location on Bosphorus, many buses pass through Ortakoy. From Taksim it takes about 15 minutes by bus. From Sultanahmet you should first take the tram to Kabatas and then either walk about 30

minutes along the coast or take a bus. You can take many buses in the direction of the Bosphorus with Ortakoy name on its sign panel.

Normally, sea access is the best way of transportation in Istanbul. Unfortunately, there is no way to go to Ortakoy by sea except once a day Bosphorus ferries and sea taxi. Besiktas is more central than Ortakoy. You can take ferries from main districts of Istanbul such as Kadikoy, Eminonu, Uskudar to Besiktas and than walk to Ortakoy in 10-15 minutes, or take a taxi(costs about 2euro)

Besiktas Travel Guide

Besiktas is one of the older neighborhoods of Istanbul though not many historic buildings has survived. It is located on the Bosphorus surrounded by Kabatas, Ortakoy and Taksim districts. If you are looking for a local rather than touristic trip, Besiktas would be one of the places with easy access, along withKadikoy.

It is said that the word 'Besiktas' is the result of the transformation of the word 'Bes Tas' which means 'five stones'. The most famous admiral of the Ottoman Empire, Barbaros Hayreddin Pasha built five stone pillars as ship moorings hence the name Bestas. In time, the name Bestas turned into Besiktas which literally means 'cradle stone'.

Barbaros Hayrettin Pasha built a waterside residence for himself in Besiktas and stayed there during his visits to Istanbul. He also built a mosque, a madrasah and a primary school in this area. When he died in 1546, he was burried in a mausolem constructed by Mimar Sinan.

Things to Do in Besiktas
Besiktas Bazaar in the main attraction of Besiktas. You can find cheap cloths, fresh fish and vegetables in this marketplace (open bazaar). Inexpensive fish restaurants and meatball eateries (Kofteci in Turkish) are abundant especially around the fish market area.

You can also taste local cuisine in the restaurants which offer home cooked Turkish meals. These restaurants are very small but they are mostly clean and reliable. For example Balkan Restaurant, also preferred by students, is a good one in this category. Towards the end of the Bazaar street there are nice pubs and bars you can enjoy.

Its football team, Besiktas Gymnastics Club (Besiktas Jimnastik Kulubu), is very important for this neighborhood. It is one of the oldest sports clubs of Turkey, founded in 1903. The football team wears black and white shirts and is nicknamed the Black Eagles and Besiktas is full of black and white flags, Black Eagle logos and statues. The club's 33,000-seat BJK Inonu Stadium which is on the most scenic stadiums in the world being on the Bosphorus seafront, southwest of the center of Besiktas. Especially on match days this area is very crowded.

You can do a Bosphorus cruise starting from Besiktas either by municipality boats or much more frequent private boats (known as 'motor' in Turkish). Most of the cruises last an hour or an hour and a half.

Besides this stadium, Istanbul Maritime Museum (Istanbul Deniz Muzesi), Dolmabahce Palace and Sinan Pasha Mosque are among other places of interest in Besiktas.

How to Go to Besiktas
Besiktas is one of the transportation hubs of Istanbul. We will not go as far to say all roads lead to Besiktas, that distinction belonging to Taksim, but it surely is pretty central.

Eminonu Travel Guide

Eminonu is the mirror of Istanbul, it reflects the complexity of this amazing city. It is the transport hub of the city where bus, rail, tram and ferries connect. Probably, 'cosmopolitan chaos' would best describe Eminonu. In daytime, you can see all kinds of people hurrying on the streets of Eminonu: enthusiastic tourists from all around the world, insistent salesmen, bargain huntingshoppers, hurried commuters, singing beggars... And of course pidgeons in front of Yenicami mosque. At night, apart from Sirkeci area where the hotels are, it is deserted.

Formerly it was an independant municipal district of Istanbul, Eminonu is now a neighbourhood of Fatih district. From the beginning, Eminonu has always been a trade hub. Therefore its resident population is low (around 30.000) but with around 2 million population in daytime it is the most crowded area of Istanbul. In Byzantium and than Ottoman Empire periods, Eminonu port was the shipping center of Istanbul. Thanks to the construction of railways and building of Sirkeci Train Station serving trains to European destinations, it has further gained importance.

Things to Do in Eminonu
It is thought that Eminonu is the place where Byzantium was founded. Eminonu is home to Spice Market,Rustem Pasha Mosque, Yenicami Mosque,

Galata bridge that connects Eminonu to Karakoy over the Golden Horn among many other sights.

A 10-15 minutes walk up the hill from Eminonu, Sultanahmet hosts many of Istanbul's highlights such asTopkapi Palace, Hagia Sophia, Blue Mosque, and Basilica Cistern,

Besides, in Sirkeci part of Eminonu, you can find various and cheap electronic goods and photography equipments at Hayyam Pasaji. In Tahtakale area, a lot of interesting handmade wooden stuff can be found. Cagaloglu is the place, the media center of Turkey until mid-1990s, now there still are some bookstores and print houses where you can buy books cheaper than other stores. Eminonu is also home for the first university of Turkey, Istanbul University. Next to this campus, with its beautiful trees, Gulhane Park where 'Tanzimat Fermani' declared is located.

Eminonu is abundant with local foods. You can find delicious Turkish doner, lahmacun or meatballs(kofte in Turkish) amog any others. The restaurants are quite small but many of them serve tasty foods. Or if you do not want spend much money on food, you can try grilled fish sandwiches, Norvegian mackarel (Balik Ekmek in Turkish) sold on the boats by the ferry dock.

How to Go to Eminonu
Eminonu is as central if not more than Taksim in terms of transportation.

You can take ferries from main districts of Istanbul such as Besiktas, Kadikoy and Uskudar. There are also car ferries to Asian-side port of Harem. For more information see ferry hours for boats serving the Bosphorus.

Tram is the another easy way of transportation to Eminonu.

Or you can also take any bus with Eminonu name on its sign panel, from almost every point of Istanbul.

Uskudar Travel Guide

Uskudar is located in the heart of the Bosphorus on the Asian side. Uskudar's history dates back to 7th century B.C. It is surrounded by Kadikoy, Beykoz and Umraniye. Once known as Scutarii, it was home to many different populations throughout history such as Athenians, Byzantium and lastly Ottoman Empire.

Now it is among the most populated areas of Istanbul with half a million people. Central Uskudar and some of its surrounding neighborhoods are very conservative.

Things to Do in Uskudar
There are a lot of places to see in and around it. Symbol of Uskudar, Maiden's Tower built on rocks out in the sea is surely among the places to be seen. There are mosques, churches and synagogues in this area. Famous mosques include Mihrimah Sultan Mosque designed by Mimar Sinan for Mihrimah Sultan, the favorite daughter of Sultan Suleyman the Magnificent and Semsi Pasha Mosque. There are close to 200 mosques in Uskudar, a few of them by famous

Ottoman architect Mimar Sinan. In addition, many historical fountains are worth seeing, such as Fountain of Ahmed III with classical Ottoman style and Fountain of Huseyin Avni Pasha with Baroque style. There are also historical residences in greater Uskudar area such as Beylerbeyi Palace a 10 minute drive to the the north, Abdulaziz Hunting Villa and Adile Sultan Pavilion and madrasahs such as Ahmediye Madrasah and Mihrimah Sultan Madrasah.

Some of the most important archeologic discoveries in Istanbul and even in Turkey were done during the construction of Marmaray an underground sea tunnel that will connect Uskudar on the Asian side to Sarayburnu, Eminonu on the European side. The construction was delayed by almost two years to unearth some of the findings from thousands of years of ago from neolithic (about 6500 years ago) and Byzantine periods in Uskudar and most importantly on European side, Yenikapi area 4th-century Port of Theodosius in Yenikapi

You can eat famous 'Kanlica Yoghurt' in Kanlica district of Uskudar about half an hour drive up the Bosphorus. Little fish restaurants on the sea offer fish at moderate or cheap prices. Although delicious, the fish sandwiches sold in Uskudar, Kadikoy and Eminonu and other corners of Istanbul is Norvegian mackarel, more appropriate to sandwiches as they are without bones and also cheap. If you are on budget and want to try local fish, we suggest fried Istavrit any day of year or Hamsi (from Septmber to July) by sitting a a small restaurant. Most importantly you can eat at Kanaat Lokantasi which offers delicious Ottoman cuisine. You can sit in the tea houses near the sea with the great view of Bosphorus and drink Turkish tea or coffee. If you want to drink alcohol you can try Turkish raki in beautiful taverns ofKuzguncuk district of Uskudar.

How to Go to Uskudar
Uskudar can easily be accessed from almost every corner of Istanbul.

Bagdat Street Istanbul

Bagdat street is a newly built posh neighborhood of Kadikoy district of Istanbul. Even though many nouveau rich live in the area, many are old and new upper middle class residents of Kadikoy, from the time when the area was a summer residence of Istanbullus back in 1940s and 1950s. Beaches of Suadiye were very popular and rich people who used to live in Taksim area would go there for the summer after an hour long trip.

Today the street is also known for secular modern Turkish residents as well as Fenerbahce fans, the biggest football club of Turkey from the same area. The rich kids of the neighborhood are still present though in less preposterous ways, and midnight street races are much less frequent.

What to Do in Bagdat Street
Bagdat street is an avenue with pedestrian traffic on both sides and it extends from Bostanci to Kadikoy.

with restaurants, cafes, bars and expensive shops of global brands.

Although it has no particular tourist attraction, it still attracts travelers who would like to spend a few calm hours strolling the street. The are around Saskinbakal and Caddebostan are the best, especially the beach strip in Caddebostan has a nice seaside park.

How to Go to Bagdat Street
You may walk to Bagdat street from Kadikoy, it starts in Kiziltoprak about 20 minutes walking distance from Kadikoy and ends in Bostanci an hour of walking later. You can also take a dolmush, bus or cab to Suadiye and walk back towards Kadikoy. You can also go to Bostanci from Kabatas (5 minutes fromTaksim by funiculaire) taking the fast ferry, also known as seabus.

Camlica Hill Istanbul

Camlica hill is the highest point of Istanbul and a good vista point. You might have noticed TV towers at the top of the hill by looking out from Galata Tower or from boats when crossing the Bopshorus. Camlica hill is about 4 kilometers from Uskudar, there are buses that go Camlica but you should ask as there are two Camlica's you should go to Buyuk Camlica (Big Camlica).

There is a Turing tea garden and restaurant which was constructed by the late Celik Guler who was interested in transforming neglected places into leisure areas. Another important Turing cafe/restaurant is in Fenerbahce. Camlica hill is only interesting for its spectacular views across of Istanbul across the Bosphorus.

Interesting facts about Istanbul

The ferry boat you see in the picture above and simit, a Turkish specialty food, oven cooked dough with sesame seeds, along with tea is the ultimate Istanbul to Turkish people.

Istanbul is dubbed by Turkish poets and Turkish people alike, the City of Seven Hills, like Rome. Interestingly

Istanbul was the capital of the Roman Empire after Rome. The city offers gorgeous views from not only from these hills but also from seaside locations.

Looking at modern Uskudar, it is hard to imagine the battle to unite Roman Empire was done in Uskudar and upon victory Roman Emperor Constantin moved the capital of the Roman Empire from Rome to Istanbul.

Sultan Ahmet was a big failure as the Sultan of the Ottoman Empire yet his name is way more popular than other great sultans such as Fatih Sultan Mehmet who conquered Istanbul or Suleyman the Magnificient who expanded the territories of the empire to its peak. The reason is Sultan Ahmet had ordered the building of Sultanahmet Mosque which rivaled St. Sophia and gave its name to the neighborhood. So once more a person of power and wealth has made his name eternal through patronage of arts. You never know how you will be remembered so it helps to support art!

Tulips, symbol of Netherlands, patsy of the Tulip Bubble, originated in Istanbul and was sent from Istanbul to Netherlands.

Our grandfathers and grandmothers living on the Asian side of Istanbul used to say 'I am going to Istanbul today' before leaving home for an hour trip to the European side of Istanbul marking the contrast between the two sides of the city. They did go to the European side mostly for compulsory reasons like, a hospital visit, business or shopping and after returning home would say things like my head is spinning.

Tea is a fairly recent national drink. It was Turkish coffee which was the national addiction but after coffee became expensive and it was possible to plant tea leaves in the Black Sea region, tea became the national drink. Turkey does not have production of coffee as it does not have a favorable climate for coffee production.

Some remains of the Great Palace of Byzantine are under Sultanahmet. In fact there are some small tunnels closed to public access but were filmed in documentaries. Remains from the Palace are mosaics in Mosaic Museum.

Needless to say the most important historical figure who has lived in Istanbul is Mustafa Kemal Ataturk who has passed away in Dolmabahce Palace, a summer residence of the president at the time. Among other famous people who have spend time in Turkey or Ottoman Empire are Kaiser Wilhelm, Franz Liszt, Florence Nightingale, Gustave Flaubert, Agatha Cristie and Pierre Loti.

Although the major Mevlevihane (whirling dervish home) is in Konya, there is one in Galata as well. Every other week, on second and fourth fridays of every month there is a sema show (whirling dervish show).

April 23th is a very special day in Turkish life. It is the children's national holiday, the only national holiday in the world dedicated to the children. But there is another celebration in Buyukada the largest of the Prince's islands: Turkish people visit Aya Yorgi church, a Byzantine Greek Orthodox church to make whishes. This was surprising even for the father of the church at the beginning as Muslim Turkish crowds would come to the church to make wishes so that they come true. Muslim scholars on that day would distribute free Kurans to inform Muslims to give up this superstition. Still, Turkish people would keep going there every year as they see it as a nonreligious activity in a church, simply a ritual to bring good luck. This was so interesting for Greek people who come to visit the church on the 28th of April that finally, a documentary movie was made about it in 2009: Bells, Threads & Miracles.

Bosphorus is where ordinary people go there fishing for food next to multimillion dollar sea side villas known as yalis.

Nisantasi is a small time Soho, in case you want to try posh shops in Istanbul with streets decorated with fancy cobbles stones and lamp posts. That's the part of city center for high income people.

Turkish society have become a class society after 30 years of neoliberal economic policies. You have the bankers, people working or doing business with multinational corporations, people tied to the state and to the governing party "du jour". And all of them tied to Wall Street. Lots of debts and lots of glamour is built since 2001. If you see in guidebooks or internet sites phrases such as "Istanbul has become hip", "In", that's why. Istanbul has always been beautiful, it is not a recent happening!

Since 1990s there is a great tendency in the Western media and guide book writers that proponents of a secular Turkish state are elite, military or intellectuals. Nothing can be further from the truth. These people have not been here long enough or have not been in enough contact with the Turkish people.

Istanbul Restaurant Guide

This guide is a collection of the restaurants which were reviewed on our monthly newsletter . Almost all restaurants and food tips are from Istanbul with a few exceptions. These no-frills, blunt reviews are done mostly by Istanbul residents who have dined in Istanbul for decades. Below you will also find a restaurant review from one of our American subscribers.

Hamdi Restaurant

A famous and old restaurant located in Eminonu, serving kebaps and mezes since decades. It has in recent years gained international fame after going through renovations.

It is a good restaurant in everything it serves but service and pushiness and we are already famous attitude is annoying. You can also buy delicious sweets and kahkes on the ground floor.

The fast service section also located at the entrance of this multi floor building with lower prices but without the view of the top floors is suggested for food enthusiasts.

TWARP rating: 7 on a scale of 10.

Haci Baba

Haci Baba is located on the busiest pedestrian street of Istanbul, Istiklal street in Beyoglu. Another great place to "see" and taste, Turkish cuisine. Packed with tourists it is a place also visited by affluent Turks, journalists etc... You can have lunch and dinner, and in summer time you can have the garden side tables overlooking the garden of the Greek Church next to it.

Unfortunately this has become another overrated restaurant with good food but with high prices and pushy service personel. Handling fame is difficult.

TWARP rating: 6 on a scale of 10.

Ciya

Ciya has become famous, yet still good. Located in Kadikoy it is the favourite restaurant for travelers who would like to taste different meals mostly from Southeast Turkey. A little high on the prices compared to the size of their servings.

There are three Ciya restaurants a few meters from each other. Two are for traditional cuisine and one for the kebaps.

<u>TWARP rating: 9 on a scale of 10.</u>

Niyazibey Iskender

If you are going to taste Iskender, a doner (gyro type but taste different than the Greek ones) with special sauce, pita bread and yogurt, this is the place! Located in Kadikoy the restaurant is not attractive in its old style design. It is just off Altiyol boulevard, only 5 minutes walking distance from the Eminonu boat station located in Kadikoy.

There are many many Iskender kebaps in Istanbul but here you can eat nicely for less 10 euros person and the best one Istanbul.

TWARP rating: 10 on a scale of 10.

Pidenem

Pide is a cousin to pizza, Turkish answer to eat cheap and well. If you would like to taste lahmacun or pide, one of the best in Istanbul is certainly Pidenem. High quality with a low price, in a nice and pretty shop located 5 minutes from Kadikoy bazaar, it is worth a try. Address: Haci Sukru sokak. No 3.

TWARP rating: 10 on a scale of 10.

Asir Restaurant

Asir formerly know as Hasir is one those restaurants without any signs, even at the entrance ! But don't go thinking that this is a really expensive one, in fact it offers cheap and nice food ! The restaurant is about one meter (3 feet) below the pavement level. Located about half a kilometer (0.3 miles) off the major pedestrian road in Istanbul, Istiklal Caddesi, Hasir offers a casual atmosphere, really nice meze (hors d'oeuvre in Turkish), fish and meat dishes.

The nicest mezes are Topik, an Armenian meze, Bomba (meaning bomb in Turkish, the name is irrelevant) extra large beans served warm, mussel salad, fava, seasoned raw fish. You can also choose the mezes from a very large selection displayed down the hall. In Turkey, if there are mezes in a restaurant that means you may consume alcoholic drinks as well, and vice-versa. Fish selection depends on season and the day, since they are bought directly from the fishermen.

Location: Parking may be a problem in the immediate vicinity. The restaurant is not in a good neigboorhood, but only 10-15 meters (yards approx.) from the Police Station and the major road crossing Taksim, making it safe.

Around USD 8-10 for a meal excluding alcoholic drinks.

TWARP rating: 7 on a scale of 10.

Pafuli Restaurant

Pafuli, is the other restaurant we have reviewed but were very frustrated about. It is the most famous restaurant in Istanbul for Black Sea regional cuisine, and it is located on the Bosphorus. The food contains too much fat, the hors d'oeuvre is not the best, except a few exceptions and the prices are quite high. The service was pretty bad as well.

TWARP rating: 3 out of 10

Kasibeyaz Restaurant

As our long time subscribers will notice, we have not talked much about kebap restaurants in Istanbul , a popular specialty of the Turkish cuisine. This time we have visited Kasibeyaz a restaurant facing the airport. A very famous stop for Istanbul dwellers, this restaurant attracts also many travelers staying in the hotel near the airport.

The hall is scaringly large and crowded: almost a few hundred visitors having their dinner in the huge dining hall. The first two things that comes to mind are the quality of service and level of noise: Surprisingly the service is excellent and the level of noise is low.

There are many appetizing starters from the Southeast region of Turkey, where the kebabs originate: cig kofte (raw meat minced many times with spices), tulum cheese, white cheese (a cousin is known as feta cheese in the US), and watermellon. Raki, wine and other drinks may accompany the starters. Then come the kebaps: Alinazik (with mashed eggplants), Adana (the basic with red pepper), Urfa (mild without hot spices), Lamb shish and many more...

The suggested desert is Kunefe, a delicious sweet with cheese served hot.

All of the above including drinks around USD 15-20 per person.

<u>TWARP rating : 9 out of 10.</u>

Caleb Gray

" A Gem of a Restaurant in Sultanahmet "- by Joe Switz

Having just returned to the U.S.A. from a month in Turkey, I'm happy to report that all you may have heard about the excellence of Turkish Cuisine is true! In general Turkish food is tasty, varied, fresh, easy to like, amply portioned and above all moderately priced. There is, however, a noticeable similarity in the dishes prepared by many of the restaurants. A marvelous exception to this sameness can be found in the CENNET RESTAURANT. Located on the street that the tram runs on about 6-7 small blocks west of the Hippodrome. (I was told that the old building that the restaurant occupies was once a Turkish bath, perhaps part of the historic Cemberlitas Bath that is still in operation and a must!)

As you enter the restaurant linger in the doorway for a few moments and soak up the visual joys of the place: The lucious assortment of meze/appertizers/salads on the table to your left; the profusion of pillows, carpets, low tables and stools scattered about the place; the three chatting ladies in their typical Turkish/Anatolian attire on the raised island in the center of the room busily preparing Gozleme the speciality of the house (the best crepes you've ever eaten!); and if your timing is right the exotic sight and sounds of Turkish music played on exotic instruments by the costumed resident musicians. Definitely not your run of the mill eateries.

O. K. Now your ready to go in. Find a pillow, rug, stool that fits your frame and feast on their simple, delicious food. As I recall there are only three types of Gozleme to choose from so choose all three; they are that delicious! My favorite, favorite was the potato gozleme. Of course chay (tea) must be consumed with the meal!

Linger and continue to enjoy the ambiance. But save room for the greatest pleasure that comes at the end of your evening when you are finally presented with the bill. So much pleasure for so litttle money!

I really can't take credit for discovering this gem of a restaurant. The credit goes to my young friend Adnan, an employee of the charming Hotel Historia where I stay when I am in Istanbul.

A Vegetarian Cafe/Restaurant: Parsifal

Turkish cuisine offers a great selection of dishes for the vegetarians so a dedicated vegetarian restaurant is not really needed for travelers to Turkey. The food is simply great and you may need a diet after you return home :) But if you would like to eat low fat vegetarian and you are on the most famous pedestrian (occasional traffic) street, Istiklal Caddesi, you may try a newly opened cafe in a side street, Parsifal for a change.

The menu is small and international dishes are majority. In most of the small, family run restaurants in Turkey, a menu does not mean much since the food selection may change daily. So check the small chalk board.

Salads are very refreshing and the soup is great. Main course include one or two non-vegetarian dish selections just in case. After you ask the bill you will be brought small gravel-like thingies in a very small cup. You may eat them, in fact you'll love them. They are "Marmara Cakili", a candy made of fruit in the inside.

TWARP rating: 8 on 10.

Konyali, located in Topkapi Palace

Konyali offers a wonderful view of the Bosphorus which separates the two continents and superb specialties of Turkish cuisine. This restaurant is packed with tourists as the tour guests are offered lunch at Konyali. It is expensive by Turkish standarts, about USD 25-40 per person for a good meal but may well be worth the extra money. If you can't afford it you still can buy sandwitches and contemplate the view while eating.

Konyali has also a great sweet shop located right next to the railway station in Eminonu. If you are into sweets, this is the place to taste some of the finest in Turkey. The walls are decorated with the pictures of famous figures who have visited Konyali, from heads of state to Kings and Queens.

Restaurants in other cities:

Restaurants in the Aegean

North and Central west Aegean is the most important place for fishing farms. In addition to the crop collected by fishermen out in the sea, there is a big supply of fish from the farms. One can spot these farms especially along the coast of Cesme peninsula.

The first thing you will notice in most of the fish restaurants is that the fish price is negotiable. And you should bargain before you walk into the restaurant. "Karagoz", "Mercan", "tekir", are moderately priced, while "Barbunya", "Swordfish", "Sinarit" and big size "Mercan" are high price items. Please note that the higher prices are mostly for fish caught by fishermen.

Most of the fish restaurants are also by the sea and offer great views, and a beautiful sunset. So if you would like to follow the Turkish dining tradition, get a table before the sunset, order a wine or even more typical, a raki (an alcoholic drink very widely consumed in Turkey) and some hors d'oeuvres. There are many cold and warm hors d'oeuvres you may order, among them squids (kalamar), octopus salad and shrimps.

Salads are dressed by olive oil, characteristic of the region, and lemon juice, the most typical, and probably the best dressing.

Depending on where you are, a busy tourist district or calm village the cost of a meal will change from USD 12-18 per person excluding drinks.

A Fish Restaurant in Ayvacik (near Assos): Hasanaki

Hasanaki, the most famous fish restaurant in the whole region is on the beach, among the camping sites around Ayvacik. The name Hasanaki is a Greekized Turkish name Hasan. The restaurant is on the highway running parallel to the sea. If you are in the area it sure is worth a visit and for directions just ask anyone, almost everyone in the area would know it. People even drive 5-6 hours from Istanbul just to eat there.

Why this place is so famous ?

It is on the beach, tables are placed at the sunset on the sand beach, a few feet from the waves silently licking the shore. The fish is fresh out of the water, daily catches of local fishermen, the hors d'oeuvre made with octopus, squids, shrimps are delicious. Vegetables grown in neighbooring farms. Salads are dressed with the classic Mediterranean beauty, extra virgin olive oil and lemon juice.

Istanbul Nightlife

There are two types of nightlife in Istanbul: Turkish and Western. Turkish nightlife involves turku bars where they play turkish folk music, live performance bars for famous Turkish singer and belly dancing shows.

When it comes to Western style you have everything you can find in a major Western capital, bars, discos, nightclubs, clubs, revues.

Taksim area is the place for nightlife, Istiklal street and then then there are clubs and bars along the Bosphorus strip.

Needless to say there are other nighlife venues outside Taksim and Bosphorus strip but they are not as concentrated. Taksim Beyoglu area by far offers the most alterntives. Vista are great at some rooftop bars and restaurants whether they are hotel roofs or private apartment building rooftops. Some of them in the Odakule area, midway between Tunel and Taksim offers some of the amazing views over the Bosphorus and the Old Town.

Events and Festivals in Istanbul

Istanbul has become a center of attraction for both reknowned and aspiring artists, fimmakers, singers. Almost all the big names in music have given concerts in Istanbul. Sometimes soon to be world famous artists like Nora Jones had given a concert in Istanbul before becoming global stars.

In addition to singers and musicians, Istanbul Film festival that takes place since almost three decades attracts famous directors and actors such as John Malkovich, Harvey Keitel, Sofia Loren and the young and established directors of cinema including Ozon.

Istanbul Bienal held every two years attracts painters, architects, installation artists from around the world.

There are also many attractive concert halls and concert venues. The most distinguished of them being St. Irene Museum, a Byzantine church hosting classical music concerts during Istanbul music festival. Other interesting concert halls and venues to hold art events and concerts are AKM (Ataturk Cultural Center) located right in Taksim Square, Cemal Resit Rey Music Hall in Harbiye, Acik Hava Tiyatrosu an open air music festival ground also in Harbiye and Kurucesme Park right on the Bosphorus. Kucukciftlik Park and Santralistnul are the other important venues for concerts and shows.

Many of these events, festivals and upcoming concert lists can be seen at IKSV Istanbul Culture and Art Foundation.

In addition, there are many smaller scale music festivals taking place year around, hosting Jazz, Rock, Classical Music concerts. Music lovers and professionals in Istanbul come together in garaj.org online Turkish music community.

The list of events stated below are only a selection of the year around Istanbul activities and it may be a pleasant surprise to find your favorite artist performing in Istanbul. Do not forget to check upcoming events and concerts before traveling to Istanbul!

Climate

Istanbul has a temperate oceanic climate which is influenced by a continental climate, with hot and humid summers and cold, wet and occasionally snowy winters.

Istanbul has a high annual average rainfall of 844mm (which is more than that of London, Dublin or Brussels, whose negative reputation Istanbul does not suffer), with late autumn and winter being the wettest, and late spring and summer being the driest. Although late spring and summer are relatively dry when compared to the other seasons, rainfall is significant during these seasons, and there is no dry season as a result.

If there is a negative reputation that Istanbul does suffer from, it is the high annual relative humidity, especially during winter and summer with the accompanying wind chill and concrete-island effect during each respective season.

Summer is generally hot with averages around 27ºC during the day and 18ºC at night. High relative humidity levels and the 'concrete-island effect' only make things worse. Expect temperatures of up to 35°C for the hottest days of the year. Summer is also the driest season, but it does infrequently rain. Showers tend to last for 15-30 minutes with the sun usually reappearing again on the same day. Flash floods are a common occurrence after heavy rainfalls (especially during summer), due to the city's hilly topography and inadequate sewage systems.

Winter is cold and wet, averaging 2ºC at night and 7ºC during the day. Although rarely below freezing during the day, high relative humidity levels and the wind chill makes it feel bitterly cold and very unpleasant.

Snowfall, which occurs almost annually, is common between the months of December and March, with an annual total snow cover of almost three weeks, but average winter snowfall varies considerably from year to year, and snow cover usually remains only for a few days after each snowfall, even under intense snow conditions.

Late spring (late May to early June) and early autumn (late September to early October) are very pleasant and therefore the best times to visit the city. During these periods it is neither cold nor hot, and still sunny, though the nights can be chilly and rain is common.

For visitors an umbrella is recommended during spring, autumn and winter, and during the summer to avoid the sun and occasionally the rain. However, it's not such a big problem, since streets of Istanbul are suddenly filled by umbrella sellers as soon as it starts raining. Although the umbrellas they provide are a little shoddy, going rate is only TRY5 –about USD3- per umbrella (though you can find much better umbrellas for that price at shops if you look around a bit).

Light clothing is recommended during summer and a light jacket and/or light sweater if the summer evenings do become chilly, warm clothing is essential during winter and a mixture of the two during spring and autumn.

Also take note that due to its huge size, topography and maritime influences, Istanbul exhibits a multitude of distinct micro-climates. Thus, different sections of Istanbul can experience different weather conditions at the same time. For example, at the same moment, it can be heavily raining in Sarıyer in the north, mildly raining in Levent (northern terminus of metro line), while Taksim, the southern terminus of metro line, is having a perfectly sunny day.

The End

www.ingramcontent.com/pod-product-compliance
Lightning Source LLC
Chambersburg PA
CBHW031103080526
44587CB00011B/806